A GIFT FOR

PEG SAMPLES

FROM

The Heavens Proclaim His Glory
© 2010 by Thomas Nelson, Inc.®

Published in Nashville, Tennessee, by Thomas Nelson. Thomas Nelson is a registered trademark of Thomas Nelson, Inc.

Designed by Koechel Peterson Design, Minneapolis, MN

Thomas Nelson, Inc., titles may be purchased in bulk for educational, business, fund-raising, or sales promotional use. For information, please e-mail SpecialMarkets@ThomasNelson.com.

ISBN-13: 978-1-4041-7502-0

Printed in China

10 11 12 13 14 [HH] 6 5 4 3 2 1

THE
heavens
PROCLAIM HIS GLORY

CREATED AND COMPILED BY LISA STILWELL

THOMAS NELSON
Since 1798

NASHVILLE   DALLAS   MEXICO CITY   RIO DE JANEIRO   BEIJING

OH MAGNIFY
THE LORD
WITH ME,
AND LET US
EXALT HIS NAME
TOGETHER.

Oh magnify the Lord with me, and let us exalt His name together.

That's the invitation of Psalm 34:3, and that's the invitation of this book. No prior generation has been afforded such a window on the universe as we now have, thanks to the Hubble Space Telescope (HST). Since slipping into its orbital groove twenty years ago, the HST has sent back thousands of eye-popping pictures that magnify the heavens beyond anything human eyes have previously observed.

This book contains some of the most beautiful of Hubble's 700,000 snapshots. Here you'll discover the splendor of a billion diamond-stars and the astonishing colors of distant planets, galaxies, and nebulae. As we see the heavens proclaiming His glory, we proclaim with the Virgin Mary, "My soul magnifies the Lord, and my spirit has rejoiced in God my Savior" (Luke 1:46).

Saying that the cosmos—with its fine-tuned complexity and undeniable beauty—is the result of some kind of random and uncaused explosion in a primordial vacuum is as preposterous as saying that the Hubble Space Telescope was assembled when a cyclone hit a glass factory. The HST took years to design and construct. It's a masterpiece of engineering and astronomic brilliance. Yet even the Hubble appears primitive compared to the complexity of the heavens it displays so beautifully for us. The more we discover, the more we're amazed. No wonder more and more scientists are affirming that the universe cannot be explained apart from an intelligent Creator.

This Creator is also our Savior, for "all things were made through Him, and without Him nothing was made that was made. In Him was life, and the life was the light of men . . ." ". . . and the name of the Lord Jesus was magnified" (John 1:3–4; Acts 19:17).

Turn the page and magnify the Lord with me, and let us exalt His name together.

David Jeremiah

NASA, ESA, A. Aloisi (STScI/ESA), and The Hubble Heritage (STScI/AURA)-ESA/Hubble Collaboration

Did you know?

One light-year is six trillion miles.

The Milky Way Galaxy is 100,000 light-years across.

(That's 600,000,000,000,000,000 miles.)

There are about 350,000,000,000 galaxies in the universe.

'Tis there—

Beyond the reach of earth—

That ever draws my heart away…

To wonder at the universe;

To think, to watch;

To dream, to pray.

KEVIN HARTNETT

Jet in Carina

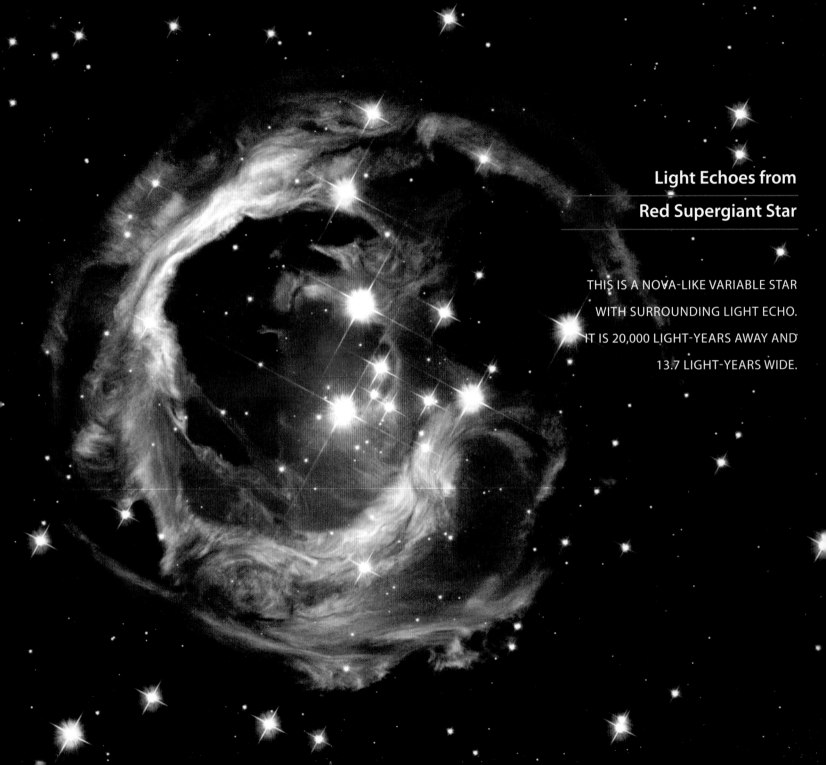

Light Echoes from
Red Supergiant Star

THIS IS A NOVA-LIKE VARIABLE STAR
WITH SURROUNDING LIGHT ECHO.
IT IS 20,000 LIGHT-YEARS AWAY AND
13.7 LIGHT-YEARS WIDE.

In the beginning God created the heavens and the earth.

GENESIS 1:1

Silently one by one, in the infinite
meadows of heaven,
Blossomed the lovely stars,
the forget-me-nots of the angels.

HENRY WADSWORTH LONGFELLOW

THE GLORIOUS DAWN OF GOD'S STORY BEGINS with the simple statement that in the beginning of time and space, God was already there. *He is eternal.* He is not bound by time or by space. *Which means He is fully present in every age, in every generation, in every corner of the Universe . . . fully present on planet Earth and on the surface of the moon . . . fully present yesterday, today, and tomorrow . . . fully present with you and with me.* EXCEPT FOR ONCE, when He "made Himself nothing, taking the very nature of a servant, being made in human likeness. *And being found in appearance as a man,* He humbled Himself and became obedient to death—even death on a cross!"

ANNE GRAHAM LOTZ, *God's Story*

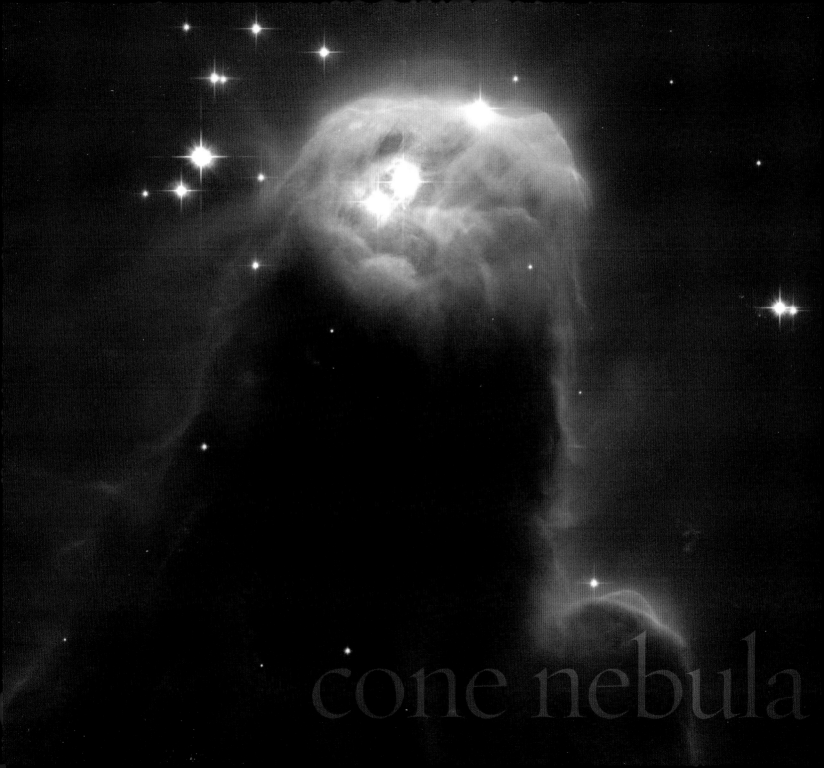
cone nebula

Then God said, "Let there be lights in the firmament of the heavens to divide the day from the night; and let them be for signs and seasons, and for days and years; and let them be for lights in the firmament of the heavens to give light on the earth"; and it was so.

GENESIS 1:14–15

How could so much have evolved out of nothing? How did the stars get scattered across such a vast expanse of space? Why is there such diversity among them? What set the stars ablaze, and where did the planets come from?

Genesis 1 gives a simple answer: God made them all. He spoke them into existence. Their vastness, their complexity, their beauty, and their sheer number all reveal the glory and the wisdom of an all-powerful Creator. And they remind us how amazing it is that such a great Creator would lavish His grace and favor on the human race. After all, from the perspective of size, our whole world constitutes only an infinitesimal speck in the vastness of all He created.

JOHN MACARTHUR, *The Battle for the Beginning*

Omega Swan Nebula

RESEMBLING THE FURY OF A RAGING SEA, THIS IMAGE ACTUALLY SHOWS A BUBBLY OCEAN OF GLOWING HYDROGEN GAS AND SMALL AMOUNTS OF OTHER ELEMENTS, SUCH AS OXYGEN AND SULFUR. IT IS 5,500 LIGHT-YEARS AWAY, LOCATED IN THE CONSTELLATION SAGITTARIUS. IT IS ROUGHLY 3 LIGHT-YEARS ACROSS.

The Majestic Sombrero Galaxy

THIS GALAXY'S HALLMARK IS A BRILLIANT WHITE,

BULBOUS CORE ENCIRCLED BY THE THICK DUST

LANES COMPRISING THE SPIRAL STRUCTURE OF

THE GALAXY. AS SEEN FROM EARTH, THE GALAXY

IS TILTED NEARLY EDGE-ON. THIS BRILLIANT

GALAXY WAS NAMED THE SOMBRERO BECAUSE

OF ITS RESEMBLANCE TO THE BROAD RIM AND

HIGH-TOP OF THE MEXICAN HAT. THE GALAXY

IS 50,000 LIGHT-YEARS ACROSS AND 28 MILLION

LIGHT-YEARS FROM EARTH.

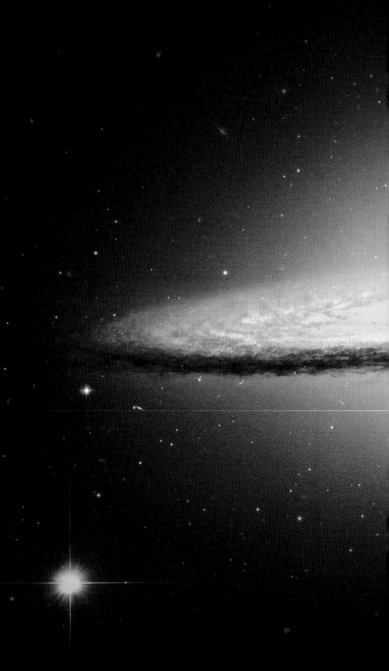

I can see how it might be possible for a man
to look down upon the earth and be an atheist,
but I cannot conceive how he could

look up into the heavens and say there is no God.

ABRAHAM LINCOLN

Saturn Aurora

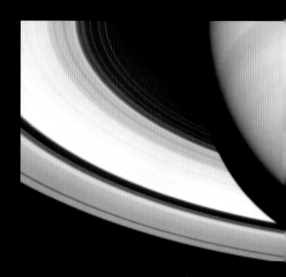

THE SEMI-MAJOR AXIS OF SATURN'S ORBIT ABOUT THE SUN IS 9.5 ASTRONOMICAL UNITS OR ROUGHLY 1.4 BILLION KILO-METERS. THE PLANET (WITHOUT RINGS) HAS A DIAMETER OF ROUGHLY 75,000 MILES AT THE EQUATOR.

By showing us the heavens,
Jesus is showing us
his Father's workshop. . . .

MAX LUCADO, *Hope Pure & Simple*

Saturn from 1996 to 2000

AS SATURN TAKES ITS 29-YEAR JOURNEY AROUND THE SUN, ITS TILT ALLOWS US TO SEE
ITS RINGS FROM DIFFERENT PERSPECTIVES. SATURN'S TILT ALSO GIVES IT SEASONS.
THE LOWEST IMAGE ON THE LEFT SHOWS THE NORTHERN HEMISPHERE'S AUTUMN,
WHILE THE UPPERMOST RIGHT IMAGE SHOWS THE WINTER.

NASA and The Hubble Heritage Team (STScI/AURA) | Acknowledgement: R.G. French (Wellesley College), J. Cuzzi (NASA/Ames), L. Dones (SwRI), and J. Lissauer (NASA/Ames)

THE LORD BY WISDOM
FOUNDED THE EARTH;
BY UNDERSTANDING
HE ESTABLISHED THE HEAVENS.

PROVERBS 3:19

THIS GALAXY IS 69 MILLION LIGHT-YEARS AWAY IN THE CONSTELLATION ERIDANUS.

Why would God create more than 350,000,000,000 galaxies (and this is a conservative estimate) that generations of people never saw or even knew existed? Do you think maybe it was to make us say, "Wow, God is unfathomably big"? Or perhaps God wanted us to see these pictures so that our response would be, "Who do I think I am?"

FRANCIS CHAN, *Crazy Love*

Galaxy NGC 1300

When I consider Your heavens,

the work of Your fingers,

The moon and the stars,

which You have ordained,

What is man

that You are mindful of him,

And the son of man

that You visit him?

PSALM 8:3–4

Globular Cluster M4

IS THE OLDEST KNOWN PLANET IDENTIFIED AND

IS ROUGHLY 5,600 LIGHT-YEARS FROM THE EARTH.

I SPEAK TO YOU FROM DEEPEST HEAVEN.

YOU HEAR ME IN THE DEPTHS OF YOUR BEING.

"Deep calls unto deep" (PSALM 42:7).

SARAH YOUNG

This is what the LORD says:

"Heaven is my throne,

and the earth is my footstool.

Could you build me a temple as good as that?

Could you build me such a resting place?

My hands have made both heaven and earth;

they and everything in them are mine.

I, the LORD, have spoken!"

ISAIAH 66:1–2 NLT

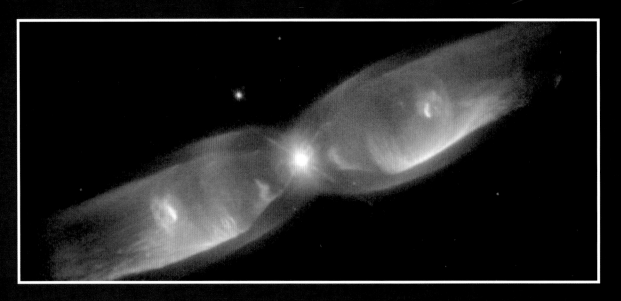

M2-9 IS A STRIKING EXAMPLE OF A "BUTTERFLY" OR A BIPOLAR PLANETARY NEBULA. ANOTHER MORE REVEALING NAME MIGHT BE THE "TWIN JET NEBULA." IF THE NEBULA IS SLICED ACROSS THE STAR, EACH SIDE OF IT APPEARS MUCH LIKE A PAIR OF EXHAUSTS FROM JET ENGINES. INDEED, BECAUSE OF THE NEBULA'S SHAPE AND THE MEASURED VELOCITY OF THE GAS, IN EXCESS OF 200 MILES PER SECOND, ASTRONOMERS BELIEVE THAT THE DESCRIPTION AS A SUPER SUPERSONIC JET EXHAUST IS QUITE APT. GROUND-BASED STUDIES HAVE SHOWN THAT THE NEBULA'S SIZE INCREASES WITH TIME, SUGGESTING THAT THE STELLAR OUTBURST THAT FORMED THE LOBES OCCURRED JUST 1,200 YEARS AGO.

WE KNOW ABOUT BEAUTY BECAUSE GOD,
THE ULTIMATE FIRST CAUSE OF EVERYTHING,
IS ALSO BEAUTIFUL... TO THE HUMBLE
AND WORSHIPFUL OF HEART... EVERY TINY PIECE
OF CREATION REMINDS THEM OF THE MAGNIFICENT
GENIUS WHO FASHIONED IT ALL.
NO ITEM OF CREATION, BE IT EVER SO BEAUTIFUL,
CAN CONVEY THE INFINITE BEAUTY OF THE SOURCE.

KEVIN HARTNETT

Splendor and majesty are before Him;
Strength and beauty are in His sanctuary.

PSALM 96:6

Barred Spiral Galaxy NGC 1512 in Many Wavelengths

THIS COLOR-COMPOSITE IMAGE WAS CREATED FROM SEVEN IMAGES TAKEN WITH THREE DIFFERENT HUBBLE CAMERAS. THE GALAXY'S CORE IS UNIQUE FOR ITS STUNNING 2,400 LIGHT-YEAR-WIDE CIRCLE OF INFANT STAR CLUSTERS, CALLED A "CIRCUMNUCLEAR" STARBURST RING. *STARBURSTS* ARE EPISODES OF VIGOROUS FORMATION OF NEW STARS AND ARE FOUND IN A VARIETY OF GALAXY ENVIRONMENTS.

*Ascribe to the L*ORD *the glory due his name;*
*worship the L*ORD *in the splendor of his holiness.*

PSALM 29:2 NIV

WHAT IS IT TO GLORIFY GOD?

To glorify God is to set God highest in our thoughts, and to have a venerable esteem of him. There is in God all that may draw forth both wonder and delight; there is a constellation of all beauties; he is *prima causa*, the original and spring-head of being, who sheds a glory upon the creature. We glorify God when we are God-admirers; [when we] admire his attributes, which are the glistering beams by which the divine nature shines forth; . . . the noble effects of his power and wisdom in making the world, which is called "the work of his fingers."

THOMAS WATSON, *A Body of Divinity*

GOD HAS RECORDED HIS GLORY UPON
THE PARCHMENT OF THE HEAVENS.
I STAND IN WONDER AND AWE AT WHAT
HE HAS WRITTEN THERE.

DR. RICHARD LEE

Butterfly Emerges from Stellar Demise
in Planetary Nebula NGC 6302

WHAT RESEMBLE DAINTY BUTTERFLY WINGS ARE ACTUALLY ROILING CAULDRONS OF GAS HEATED TO MORE THAN 36,000 DEGREES FAHRENHEIT. THE GAS IS TEARING ACROSS SPACE AT MORE THAN 600,000 MILES AN HOUR—FAST ENOUGH TO TRAVEL FROM EARTH TO THE MOON IN 24 MINUTES! NGC 6302 LIES WITHIN OUR MILKY WAY GALAXY, ROUGHLY 3,800 LIGHT-YEARS AWAY IN THE CONSTELLATION SCORPIUS. THE "BUT-TERFLY" STRETCHES FOR MORE THAN TWO LIGHT-YEARS, WHICH IS ABOUT HALF THE DISTANCE FROM THE SUN TO THE NEAREST STAR, ALPHA CENTAURI.

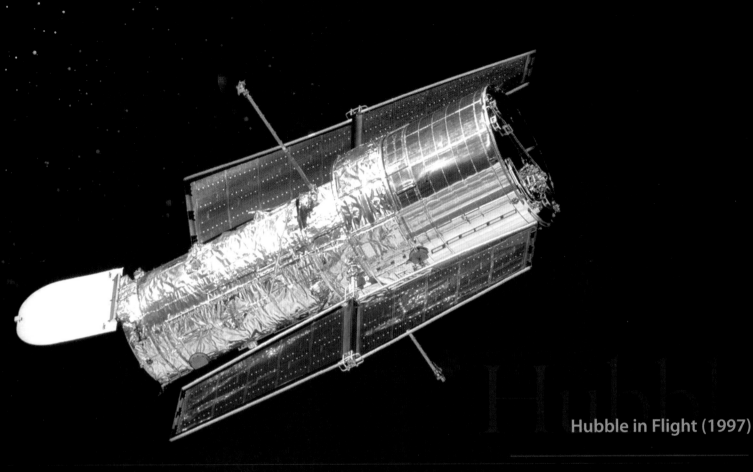

Hubble in Flight (1997)

THE HUBBLE SPACE TELESCOPE DRIFTS THROUGH SPACE IN THIS PICTURE, TAKEN BY
SPACE SHUTTLE DISCOVERY DURING HUBBLE'S SECOND SERVICING MISSION IN 1997.
THE 10-FOOT APERTURE DOOR, OPEN TO ADMIT LIGHT, CLOSES TO BLOCK OUT SPACE
DEBRIS. THE OBSERVATORY'S SOLAR PANELS AND FOIL-LIKE THERMAL BLANKETS ARE
CLEARLY VISIBLE. THE SOLAR PANELS PROVIDE POWER, WHILE THE THERMAL BLANKETS
PROTECT HUBBLE FROM THE EXTREME TEMPERATURES OF SPACE.

THE HUBBLE SPACE TELESCOPE is a space-based telescope that was launched in 1990 by the space shuttle. From its position 380 miles above the Earth's surface, the HST has expanded our understanding of star birth, star death, and galaxy evolution, and has helped move black holes from theory to fact. In its first 15 years, the telescope recorded over 700,000 images. The telescope's instruments are the astronomer's eyes to the universe.

Carina Nebula

Carina Nebula

THIS IS A 50-LIGHT-YEAR-WIDE VIEW OF THE CENTRAL REGION OF THE CARINA NEBULA WHERE A MAELSTROM OF STAR BIRTH—AND DEATH—IS TAKING PLACE. THE FANTASY-LIKE LANDSCAPE OF THE NEBULA IS SCULPTED BY THE ACTION OF OUTFLOWING WINDS AND SCORCHING ULTRAVIOLET RADIATION FROM THE MONSTER STARS THAT INHABIT THIS INFERNO. IN THE PROCESS, THESE STARS ARE SHREDDING THE SURROUNDING MATERIAL THAT IS THE LAST VESTIGE OF THE GIANT CLOUD FROM WHICH THE STARS WERE BORN. THE IMMAENSE NEBULA CONTAINS AT LEAST A DOZEN BRILLIANT STARS THAT ARE ROUGHLY ESTIMATED TO BE AT LEAST 50 TO 100 TIMES THE MASS OF OUR SUN. IT IS AN ESTIMATED 7,500 LIGHT-YEARS AWAY.

These are the magnets which so strongly move

And work all night upon thy light and love,

As beauteous shapes, we know not why,

Command and guide the eye.

HENRY VAUGHAN, FROM *The Star*

Come and see what God has done,
how awesome his works in man's behalf!

PSALM 66:5 NIV

Hubble Captures Full View of Uranus's Rings on Edge: Unannotated

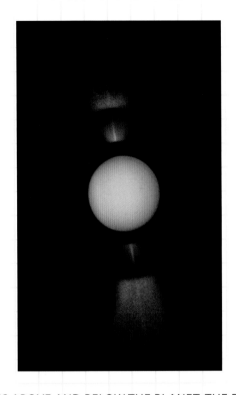

THE EDGE-ON RINGS APPEAR AS SPIKES ABOVE AND BELOW THE PLANET. THE RINGS CANNOT BE SEEN RUNNING FULLY ACROSS THE FACE OF THE PLANET BECAUSE THE BRIGHT GLARE OF THE PLANET HAS BEEN BLOCKED OUT IN THE HST PHOTO (A SMALL AMOUNT OF RESIDUAL GLARE APPEARS AS A FAN-SHAPED IMAGE ARTIFACT, ALONG WITH AN EDGE BETWEEN THE EXPOSURE FOR THE INNER AND OUTER RINGS). EARTHBOUND ASTRONOMERS ONLY SEE THE RINGS' EDGE EVERY 42 YEARS AS THE PLANET FOLLOWS A LEISURELY 84-YEAR ORBIT ABOUT THE SUN. HOWEVER, THE LAST TIME THE RINGS WERE TILTED EDGE-ON TO EARTH, ASTRONOMERS DIDN'T EVEN KNOW THEY EXISTED.

THE BIG BANG POSTULATES THAT BILLIONS OF YEARS AGO THE UNIVERSE BEGAN AS AN INFINITELY DENSE POINT CALLED A SINGULARITY AND HAS BEEN EXPANDING EVER SINCE. THOUGH THE BIG BANG IS NOT TAUGHT IN THE BIBLE, IT LENDS SCIENTIFIC SUPPORT TO THE SCRIPTURAL TEACHING THAT GOD CREATED THE UNIVERSE *ex nihilo* (out of nothing).

First, like the Bible, the Big Bang postulates that the universe had a beginning. As such, it stands in stark opposition to the scientifically silly suggestion that the universe eternally existed, not to the biblical account of origins.

Furthermore, if the universe had a beginning it had to have a cause. Indeed, according to empirical science whatever begins to exist must have a cause equal to or greater than itself. Thus, the Big Bang flies in the face of the philosophically preposterous proposition that the universe sprang from nothing apart from an uncaused First Cause.

Finally, though evolutionists hold to Big Bang cosmology, the Big Bang does not entail biological evolution. In other words, the Big Bang theory answers questions concerning the origin of the space-time universe, as opposed to questions concerning the origin of biological life on earth.

HANK HANEGRAAFF, *Complete Bible Answer Book*

No single molecule
in the vast universe of creation
ever acts independently from
the sovereign providence of a holy God.

R. C. SPROUL

For by him all things were created;
things in heaven and on earth, visible and invisible,
whether thrones or powers or rulers or authorities;
all things were created by him and for him.
He is before all things, and in Him all things
HOLD TOGETHER.

COLOSSIANS 1:16-17 NIV

A "TRUE COLOR" MOSAIC IMAGE OF A GAS PLUME NEAR THE EDGE OF THE ORION NEBULA.

Galaxy Triplet Arp 274

TRIPLE GALAXY SYSTEM

Arp 274 is a system of three galaxies. Two of the three galaxies are forming new stars at a high rate. This is evident in the bright blue knots of star formation that are strung along the arms of the galaxy on the right and along the small galaxy on the left. The largest component is located in the middle of the three. It appears as a spiral galaxy, which may be barred. The entire system resides at about 400 million light-years away from Earth in the constellation Virgo.

What melts our hearts is not just that there is beauty in the universe.
What melts us is the knowledge that God designed all beauty
to show us who He is, as a symbolic language of the soul.
All nature is God wooing us to Himself.

STEPHEN MANSFIELD

And to think that the One

who created these magnificent heavens in the vastness of space knows each one of us seemingly insignificant creatures in a yada way! *(Yada: Hebrew word meaning "to know and be known," used in Scriptures 944 times, as in Psalm 139 to describe how intimately God knows each one of us.)* This glimpse into the heavens causes me to fall down and worship the One who loves me so. | NETA JACKSON

O Lord, You have searched me and known me.

You know my sitting down and my rising up;

You understand my thought afar off.

You comprehend my path and my lying down,

And are acquainted with all my ways.

For there is not a word on my tongue,

But behold, O Lord, You know it altogether.

You have hedged me behind and before,

And laid Your hand upon me.

Such knowledge is too wonderful for me;

It is high, I cannot attain it.

PSALM 139:1–6

Dust Band around the Nucleus of Black Eye Galaxy M64

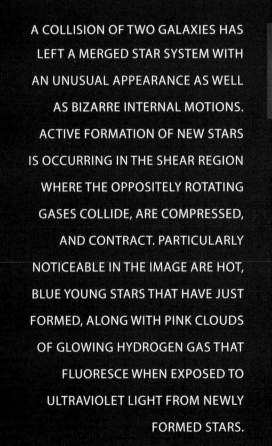

A COLLISION OF TWO GALAXIES HAS LEFT A MERGED STAR SYSTEM WITH AN UNUSUAL APPEARANCE AS WELL AS BIZARRE INTERNAL MOTIONS. ACTIVE FORMATION OF NEW STARS IS OCCURRING IN THE SHEAR REGION WHERE THE OPPOSITELY ROTATING GASES COLLIDE, ARE COMPRESSED, AND CONTRACT. PARTICULARLY NOTICEABLE IN THE IMAGE ARE HOT, BLUE YOUNG STARS THAT HAVE JUST FORMED, ALONG WITH PINK CLOUDS OF GLOWING HYDROGEN GAS THAT FLUORESCE WHEN EXPOSED TO ULTRAVIOLET LIGHT FROM NEWLY FORMED STARS.

Every beautiful created thing points
to an even more beautiful Creator.

We know about love because God is love.

We know about Fatherhood because God is a Father.

As David gazed into an unfathomably large universe,

he realized it was just finger work for God. As great as the

universe is, God is infinitely greater. And the human race

is nothing by comparison.

JOHN MACARTHUR, *The Battle for the Beginning*

The Stingray Nebula

THE STINGRAY NEBULA (HEN-1357)
IS SO NAMED BECAUSE ITS SHAPE
RESEMBLES A STINGRAY FISH. IT IS
THE YOUNGEST KNOWN PLANETARY
NEBULA. THE COLORS SHOWN
ARE ACTUAL COLORS EMITTED BY
NITROGEN (RED), OXYGEN (GREEN),
AND HYDROGEN (BLUE).

THERE IS NO NEUTRAL GROUND IN THE UNIVERSE; EVERY SQUARE INCH, EVERY SPLIT SECOND, IS CLAIMED BY GOD.

C.S. LEWIS

The LORD owns the world and everything in it—

the heavens, even the highest heavens, are his.

DEUTERONOMY 10:14 NCV

M100

Spiral Galaxy M100

AN IMAGE OF THE GRAND
DESIGN SPIRAL GALAXY M100
OBTAINED WITH THE SECOND
GENERATION WIDE FIELD AND
PLANETARY CAMERA2 (WFPC2).

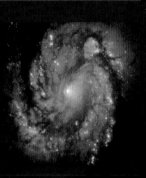
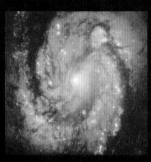
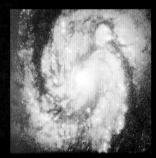

GOD INTENDS US TO ENJOY HIS CREATION; that's why it's beautiful. *We see His wonders above us, beneath us, all around us, even within us. We're encircled by an eye-popping, mind-boggling, awe-inspiring cosmos, which logically implies there's a Creator who sees, thinks, and inspires awe.* The universe is full of pulsating energy, so its Maker must be omnipotent. IT APPEARS VIRTUALLY ENDLESS, SO HE MUST BE ETERNAL. *Because it's finely calibrated, He must be intelligent.* Since it contains life, He must be personal; and since it's magnificent, He must be altogether lovely. ASSUMING THE EXISTENCE OF A CREATOR ISN'T A MINDLESS LEAP OF FAITH; *it's the most reasonable thing in the universe.* ROBERT MORGAN

The Antennae Galaxies

NGC 40038-4039

THESE ARE TWO SPIRAL GALAXIES DRAWN
TOGETHER BY GRAVITY. THEY ARE THE
NEAREST AND YOUNGEST EXAMPLES OF A
PAIR OF COLLIDING GALAXIES.

Impossibly gigantic,
Yet hid from normal view;
With silent force controlling
The sum in your purview.

And is it not these likenesses,
In beauty, strength, and grace,
That take my eye to see in you
The Great Designer's trace?

KEVIN HARTNETT

(NASA, ESA, and the Hubble Heritage Team (STScI/AURA)-ESA/Hubble Collaboration. Acknowledgment: B. Whitmore (Space Telescope Science Institute))

The Antennae Galaxies Closeup

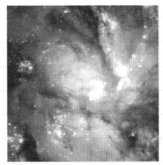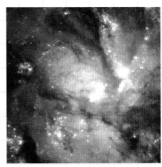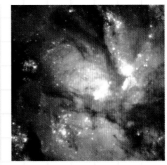

ONE THING I REALIZE EACH TIME I LOOK UPON
AN AFRICAN SUNSET, IS THAT WE ARE JUST
GRAINS OF SAND IN A MASSIVE UNIVERSE.
BUT YET HE KNOWS THE HAIRS ON OUR HEAD.
AGAIN I ASK MYSELF, HOW GREAT IS OUR GOD?

AUSTIN GUTWEIN

"But I am the LORD your God,

Who divided the sea whose waves roared—

The LORD of hosts is His name.

And I have put My words in your mouth;

I have covered you with the shadow of My hand,

That I may plant the heavens,

Lay the foundations of the earth,

And say to Zion, 'You are My people.' "

ISAIAH 51:15–16

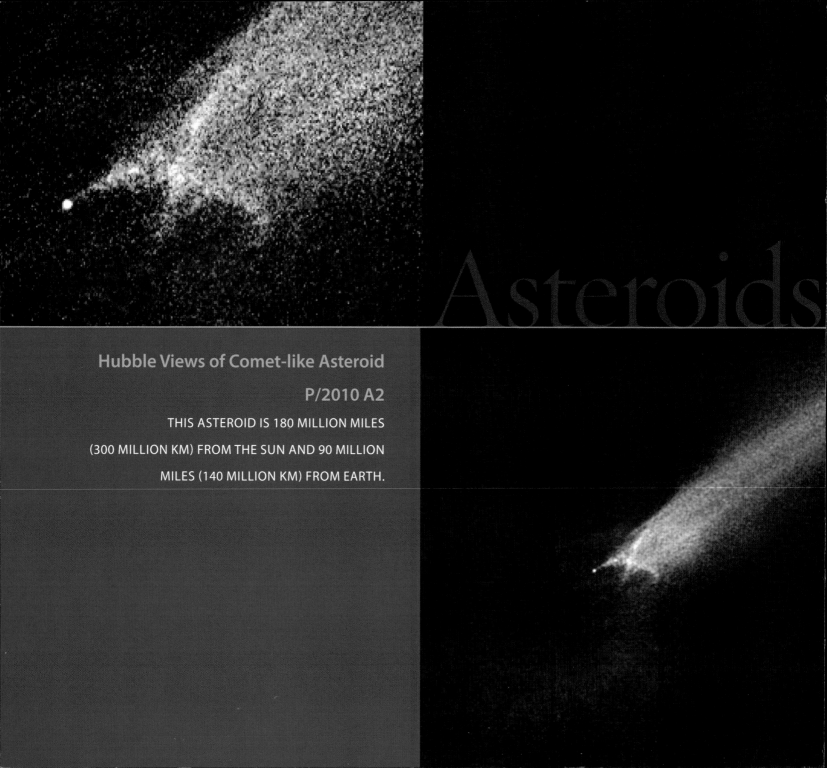

Asteroids

Hubble Views of Comet-like Asteroid

P/2010 A2

THIS ASTEROID IS 180 MILLION MILES
(300 MILLION KM) FROM THE SUN AND 90 MILLION
MILES (140 MILLION KM) FROM EARTH.

BEING A BIT OF A TELESCOPE ENTHUSIAST, I've sat up late on many a chilly night and marveled at all those *brilliant little marbles, faraway diamonds, and silvery smudges,* my mind boggled by the beauty, unable to comprehend the size, wondering at the time it took for those images to travel to my retinas. DOES IT MAKE ME FEEL SMALL? *Well, not so much as it makes me feel safe.* You see, I know their Maker, and when I consider what Mind and Power are holding it all together, I'm comforted to know Whose plan it all is and that He has made me a chosen part of it.

FRANK PERETTI

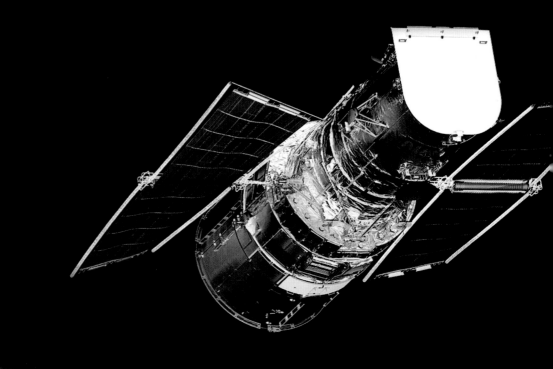

HUBBLE DRIFTS OVER EARTH AFTER ITS RELEASE ON
MAY 19, 2009 BY THE CREW OF THE SPACE SHUTTLE ATLANTIS.
THE CREW HAD PERFORMED ALL PLANNED TASKS OVER
THE COURSE OF FIVE SPACEWALKS, MAKING THE SERVICING
MISSION 4, THE FIFTH ASTRONAUT VISIT TO THE HUBBLE
SPACE TELESCOPE, AN UNQUALIFIED SUCCESS.

- Hubble is nearly the size of a large school bus, and it can fit inside the cargo bay of a space shuttle.

- Hubble whirls around Earth at 5 miles (8 KM) per second. If a car could travel that fast, a road trip from Los Angeles to New York City would take only 10 minutes.

- Hubble completes one full orbit every 97 minutes.

- In an average orbit, Hubble uses about the same amount of energy as twenty-eight 100-watt light bulbs.

- Hubble travels more than 150 million miles (241 million km) per year.

Jupiter

THERE ARE

When the Hubble Space Telescope was launched with blurred optics, *I joined the team that worked in the Neutral Buoyancy Simulator (a giant water tank) to train the astronauts going up to repair it.* I AM PROUD OF THAT WORK. The Hubble has changed the very way we understand who we, as citizens of Planet Earth, are and where we are going. *Yet, within the magnificent pictures of Hubble is a deeper truth.* THERE ARE MIRACLES EVERYWHERE ALTHOUGH SOMETIMES THEY ARE CONCEALED, NOT BY GOD, BUT BY OUR OWN EYES. *All we need to do is look, and they will be seen.*

HOMER HICKAM

MIRACLES EVERYWHERE

Cartwheel Galaxy

THE STRIKING RING-LIKE FEATURE
IS A DIRECT RESULT OF A SMALLER
INTRUDER GALAXY—POSSIBLY ONE OF
TWO OBJECTS TO THE RIGHT OF THE
RING—THAT CAREENED THROUGH THE
CORE OF THE HOST GALAXY. LIKE A ROCK
TOSSED INTO A LAKE, THE COLLISION
SENT A RIPPLE OF ENERGY INTO SPACE,
PLOWING GAS AND DUST IN FRONT OF
IT. EXPANDING AT 200,000 MPH, THIS
COSMIC TSUNAMI LEAVES IN ITS WAKE
A FIRESTORM OF NEW STAR CREATION.
HUBBLE REVEALS BRIGHT BLUE KNOTS
THAT ARE GIGANTIC CLUSTERS OF
NEWBORN STARS AND IMMENSE LOOPS
AND BUBBLES BLOWN
INTO SPACE BY EXPLODING STARS
(CALLED *SUPERNOVAE*).

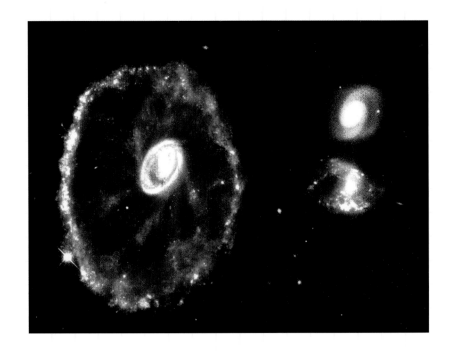

Behold the heavens
bespangled with lights.
We see God's wisdom blazing in
the sun and twinkling in the stars;
we see it in His marshalling
and ordering everything in its
proper place and sphere.

THOMAS WATSON

A Body of Divinity

NGC 5866

IS AN EDGE-ON GALAXY THAT IS TILTED TO OUR LINE-OF-SIGHT. IT IS CLASSIFIED AS AN *S0 LENTICULAR,* DUE TO ITS FLAT STELLAR DISK AND LARGE ELLIPSOIDAL BULGE. IT LIES IN THE NORTHERN CONSTELLATION DRACO AT A DISTANCE OF 44 MILLION LIGHT-YEARS. IT HAS A DIAMETER OF ROUGHLY 60,000 LIGHT-YEARS.

The next time a sunrise steals your breath or

a meadow of flowers leaves you speechless, remain that way.

Say nothing and listen as heaven whispers,

"Do you like it? I did it just for you."

MAX LUCADO, *The Great House of God*

I LIKEN VARIOUS ATTRIBUTES OF GOD TO THE QUALITIES OF A GIGANTIC SPIRAL GALAXY. BOTH ARE TOO GRAND TO FULLY COMPREHEND. AS HUGE AS OUR OWN MILKY WAY GALAXY IS, AND DESPITE THE FACT THAT IT IS SILENTLY HURLING OUR ENTIRE SOLAR SYSTEM AROUND ITS CENTER AT A SPEED FASTER THAN A BULLET'S, WE LIVE COMPLETELY UNAWARE OF ITS PRESENCE AND INFLUENCE. HOW SIMILAR THIS IS TO GOD! EVERY MOMENT OUR LIVES ARE SILENTLY GUIDED IN HIS POWERFUL SOVEREIGNTY, BUT WE DON'T EVEN KNOW IT. THEN TOO BEHOLD THE MAJESTY AND BEAUTY OF THE GALAXY'S SPECTACULAR AND MYSTERIOUS SPIRAL ARMS. ALL THESE THINGS BRING US TO BEHOLD THE GENIUS OF CREATION HIMSELF, THE GREAT DESIGNER OF ALL. | KEVIN HARTNETT

The Heart *of the* Whirlpool Galaxy

To whom, then, will
you compare God?
What image will you
compare Him to?

ISAIAH 40:18 NIV

Venus

VENUS

THIS IS AN ULTRAVIOLET-LIGHT IMAGE
OF THE PLANET VENUS, TAKEN ON
JANUARY 24, 1995, WHEN VENUS WAS
AT A DISTANCE OF 70.6 MILLION MILES
(113.6 MILLION KM) FROM EARTH.

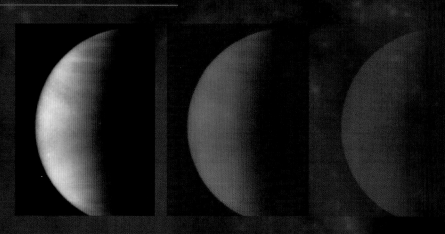

GOD'S ART SPEAKS OF HIMSELF, REFLECTING WHO HE IS AND WHAT HE IS LIKE.

The heavens declare the glory of God;
the skies proclaim the work of his hands.
Day after day they pour forth speech;
night after night they display knowledge.
There is no speech or language where their voice is not heard.
Their voice goes out into all the earth,
their words to the ends of the world.

PSALM 19:1–4 NIV

THIS IS WHY WE ARE CALLED
TO WORSHIP HIM.
HIS ART, HIS HANDIWORK,
AND HIS CREATION ALL ECHO
THE TRUTH THAT HE IS GLORIOUS.

FRANCIS CHAN, *Crazy Love*

The stars shine over the earth,

The stars shine over the sea,

The stars look up to the mighty God,

The stars look down on me;

The stars will live for a million years,

For a million years and a day!

But Christ and I shall live and love

When the stars have passed away.

ROBERT LOUIS STEVENSON

SEPTEMBER, 2002   DECEMBER, 2002   SEPTEMBER, 2006

Star V838

Omega Centauri

Astronomers are now convinced that there are more stars in the universe than there are grains of sand on the beaches of the world. When you consider that our sun—the star—is a grain of sand, this makes Earth infinitesimally small! And on this eensy speck of earth, out of the billions of people, the Lord of the universe came to earth to save you. Truly, the heavens declare not only His glory, but His mercy!

JONI EARECKSON TADA

For Your mercy is great above the heavens,
And Your truth reaches to the clouds.
Be exalted, O God, above the heavens,
And Your glory above all the earth.

PSALM 108:4–5

MY SHOW ON THE FOX NEWS CHANNEL PUTS ME IN TIMES SQUARE in New York every week, but it's not where I choose to live. *The lights are bright and dazzling, but the man-made and sometimes dizzying illumination of the city doesn't compare to the simple sights of a night sky seen from a rural and remote countryside.* Staring into the stars reminds me how small and finite I am and how grand and infinite God is. WHAT HE MADE CAN'T BE EQUALED BY TIMES SQUARE TIMES A THOUSAND.

FORMER GOVERNOR MIKE HUCKABEE

Star Cluster NGC 290

European Space Agency and NASA. | Acknowledgment: E. Olszewski (University of Arizona)

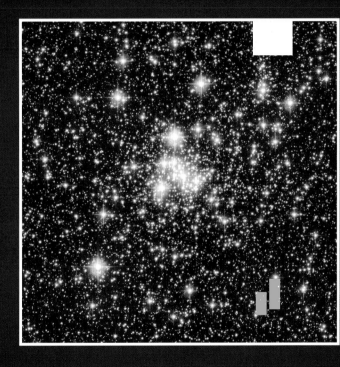

THIS STAR CLUSTER IS ABOUT 200,000 LIGHT-YEARS
AWAY. THE IMAGE IS ABOUT 65 LIGHT-YEARS WIDE.

A String of "Cosmic Pearls" Surround an Exploding Star

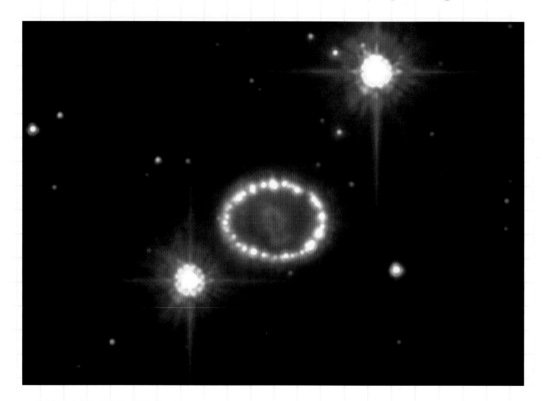

EACH STAR IN THE HEAVENS
IS DIFFERENT FROM ALL OTHERS.
LIKE FINGERPRINTS AND SNOWFLAKES,
THEY REVEAL THE VAST DIVERSITY
REFLECTED IN GOD'S CREATIVE WISDOM.

JOHN MACARTHUR

The Battle for the Beginning

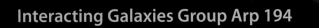

Interacting Galaxies Group Arp 194

THESE GALAXIES ARE IN
THE CONSTELLATION URSA MAJOR,
600 MILLION LIGHT-YEARS AWAY.

Can you imagine an endless view of color, comets, and sparkling curlicues pirouetting through the heavens? Lean in and be reminded that our Creator continues to shower the cosmos with His glory. These pictures and thoughts make my heart dance with joy!

PATSY CLAIRMONT

THESE SNAPSHOTS REVEAL DRAMATIC ACTIVITIES WITHIN THE CORE OF THE GALAXY NGC 3079, WHERE A LUMPY BUBBLE OF HOT GAS IS RISING FROM A CAULDRON OF GLOWING MATTER. THE PICTURE SHOWS THE BUBBLE IN THE CENTER OF THE GALAXY'S DISK. THE STRUCTURE IS MORE THAN 3,000 LIGHT-YEARS WIDE AND RISES 3,500 LIGHT-YEARS ABOVE THE GALAXY'S DISK. THE SMALLER PHOTO BELOW IS A CLOSE-UP VIEW OF THE BUBBLE. ASTRONOMERS SUSPECT THAT THE BUBBLE IS BEING BLOWN BY "WINDS" (HIGH-SPEED STREAMS OF PARTICLES) RELEASED DURING A BURST OF STAR FORMATION.

My help comes from the LORD,
who made heaven and earth.

PSALM 121:2 ESV

When life becomes overwhelming, I step outside and lift my gaze to the heavens. For I am convinced that the God who holds the stars in place will hold us through this night.

SHEILA WALSH

Galaxy Cluster MACS J0717

JESUS, KING OF ANGELS, HEAVEN'S LIGHT,
Shine Your face upon this house tonight.
Let no evil come into my dreams;
Light of heaven, keep me in Your peace.

The universe is vast beyond the stars,
But You are mindful when the sparrow falls,
And mindful of the anxious thoughts,
That find me, surround me, and bind me . . . .

With all my heart I love You, Sovereign Lord.
Tomorrow, let me love You even more.
And rise to speak the goodness of Your name
Until I close my eyes and sleep again.

"JESUS, KING OF ANGELS" BY FERNANDO ORTEGA

THIS IMAGE SHOWS THE FULL SYSTEM
OF THREE RINGS OF GLOWING GAS
SURROUNDING SUPERNOVA 1987A

The Son is the radiance of God's glory
and the exact representation of his being
sustaining all things by his powerful word.

HEBREWS 1:3 NIV

IF GOD HAS THE POWER to create and sustain the universe,
how can you or I think His power is insufficient for our daily lives?

Nothing is beyond His ability; whether it's . . .

a problem to solve,
a marriage to reconcile,
A MEMORY TO HEAL,
a guilty conscience to cleanse,
a sin to forgive,
a business to save,
A BUDGET TO STRETCH,
another mouth to feed,

a body to clothe,
A BOSS TO PLEASE,
a job to find,
a habit to break
A CAPTIVE TO FREE,
a prodigal to return,
an addiction to overcome,
or anything else we could name.

ANNE GRAHAM LOTZ
My Jesus Is Everything

UNDERSEA CORRAL? ENCHANTED CASTLES? SPACE SERPENTS? THESE EERIE, DARK, PILLAR-LIKE STRUCTURES ARE ACTUALLY COLUMNS OF COOL INTERSTELLAR HYDROGEN GAS AND DUST THAT ARE ALSO INCUBATORS FOR NEW STARS. THE TALLEST PILLAR (LEFT) IS ABOUT ABOUT 4 LIGHT-YEARS LONG FROM BASE TO TIP..

DEPEND ON THE LORD AND HIS STRENGTH;

always go to him for help.

Remember the miracles he has done;

REMEMBER HIS WONDERS AND HIS DECISIONS.

You are descendants of his servant Abraham,

the children of Jacob, his chosen people.

PSALM 105:4–6 NCV

Lagoon Nebula, M8

THIS IMAGE REVEALS A PAIR OF ONE-HALF
LIGHT-YEAR-LONG INTERSTELLAR "TWISTERS"—
EERIE FUNNELS AND TWISTED-ROPE
STRUCTURES—IN THE HEART OF THE LAGOON
NEBULA, WHICH LIES 5,000 LIGHT-YEARS
AWAY IN THE DIRECTION OF
THE CONSTELLATION SAGITTARIUS.

YES, YOU, LORD, ARE IN HEAVEN.

Yes, you rule the universe.

Yes, you sit upon the stars

and make your home in the deep.

But yes, yes, yes, you are with me.

THE LORD IS WITH ME.

The Creator is with me.

Yahweh is with me.

MAX LUCADO, *Safe in the Shepherd's Arms*

THESE GREAT CLOUDS OF COLD HYDROGEN RESEMBLE SUMMER AFTERNOON
THUNDERHEADS. THEY TOWER ABOVE THE SURFACE OF A MOLECULAR CLOUD
ON THE EDGE OF THE NEBULA. SO-CALLED "ELEPHANT TRUNK" PILLARS RESIST
BEING HEATED AND EATEN AWAY BY BLISTERING ULTRAVIOLET RADIATION FROM
THE NEBULA'S BRIGHTEST STARS.

At the planetarium inside our Creation Museum, many people ask us: how could the first three days of the Creation Week in Genesis have been 24-hour days when the Sun wasn't created until Day Four? Actually, you don't really need the Sun for day and night—all that's required is light coming from one direction. While the Bible says that God made light on Day One; He just did not tell us where the light came from. It must have been from some kind of temporary source, and then it was replaced by the Sun on Day Four.

By the way, evolutionists say that the Sun existed before the Earth, and so we tell Christians that they shouldn't accept evolutionary cosmology and try to add it to the Bible.

One of the reasons God may have left the Sun's creation until Day Four could have been due to His foreknowledge, that He knew that some future cultures would worship the Sun. By creating the Sun after the Earth, God may have been showing us that *He was the source of all power*. Ultimately, as the theologian Basil the Great declared, the Sun wasn't necessary for the day–night cycle. He added: "The sun and the moon did not yet exist, in order that those who live in ignorance of God may not consider the Sun as the origin and the father of light, or as the maker of all that grows out of the earth. That is why there was a fourth day."

Indeed, *we are to worship the God of Creation, not the creation He had made* (ROMANS 1:25).

KEN HAM

By faith we understand that the worlds were framed by the word of God, so that the things which are seen were not made of things which are visible.

HEBREWS 11:3

The Spirograph Nebula (IC 418)

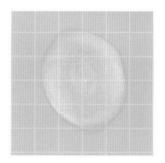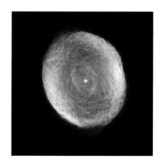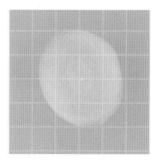

Saturn's Double Light Show

IN JANUARY AND MARCH 2009, ASTRONOMERS TOOK
ADVANTAGE OF A RARE OPPORTUNITY TO RECORD SATURN
WHEN ITS RINGS WERE EDGE-ON, RESULTING IN A UNIQUE
MOVIE FEATURING THE NEARLY SYMMETRICAL LIGHT SHOW
AT BOTH OF THE GIANT PLANET'S POLES. IT TAKES SATURN
ALMOST THIRTY YEARS TO ORBIT THE SUN, WITH THE
OPPORTUNITY TO IMAGE BOTH OF ITS POLES
OCCURRING ONLY TWICE DURING THAT TIME. THE LIGHT
SHOWS, CALLED *AURORAE*, ARE PRODUCED WHEN ELECT-
RICALLY CHARGED PARTICLES RACE ALONG THE PLANET'S
MAGNETIC FIELD AND INTO THE UPPER ATMOSPHERE WHERE
THEY EXCITE ATMOSPHERIC GASES, CAUSING THEM TO GLOW.
SATURN'S AURORAE RESEMBLE THE SAME PHENOMENA THAT
TAKE PLACE AT THE EARTH'S POLES.

Saturn

COMMON-SENSE LOGIC SUGGESTS THAT EVERY WATCH HAS A WATCHMAKER.

Every building has a builder. Every structure has an architect.

Every arrangement has a plan. Every plan has a designer.

And every design has a purpose.

We see the universe, infinitely more complex than any watch

and infinitely greater than any man-made structure,

and it is natural to conclude that Someone

infinitely powerful and infinitely intelligent made it.

"FOR SINCE THE CREATION OF THE WORLD

His invisible attributes, His eternal power and divine nature,

have been clearly seen, being understood

through what has been made" (ROMAN 1:20 NASB).

JOHN MACARTHUR, *Battle for the Beginning*

Planetary Nebula NGC 6543:
Gaseous Cocoon around a Dying Star

MYSTERIOUS STELLAR FIREWORKS CREATE

EXPANDING GAS SHELLS AND BLOWTORCH-LIKE JETS,

WHICH FORM A SPECTACULARLY INTRICATE

AND SYMMETRICAL STRUCTURE. THE NEBULA

IS A FOSSIL RECORD OF THE LATE STAGES

OF THE STAR'S EVOLUTION.

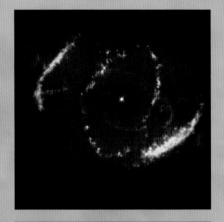

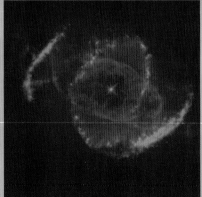

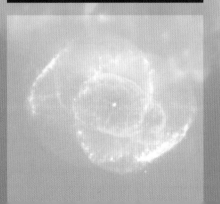

The enjoyment of God's sweet presence here

is the most contented life:

He is a hive of sweetness,

a magazine of riches, a fountain of delight.

THOMAS WATSON

A Body of Divinity

Interacting Spiral Galaxies

NGC 2207 and IC 2163

IN THE DIRECTION OF THE CONSTELLATION CANIS MAJOR,
TWO SPIRAL GALAXIES PASS BY EACH OTHER LIKE MAJESTIC SHIPS
IN THE NIGHT. STRONG TIDAL FORCES OF ONE HAVE DISTORTED THE
SHAPE OF THE OTHER, FLINGING OUT STARS AND GAS INTO LONG
STREAMERS STRETCHING OUT A HUNDRED THOUSAND LIGHT-YEARS
TOWARD THE RIGHT-HAND EDGE OF THE IMAGE.

We are reminded in Psalm 19:1, *"The heavens declare the glory of God and the firmament shows His handiwork."* The majesty of God's creation reaches far beyond what the human eye can see or comprehend. We are blessed to experience the beauty and vastness of the starry host. It is hard to imagine that God designed all this for our pleasure and for His glory.

JACK & MARSHA COUNTRYMAN

Grappling Hubble (2009)

Pointing the Hubble telescope and locking on to distant celestial targets is like holding a laser light steady on a dime that is 400 miles away.

Or, put another way . . .

In order to take images of distant, faint objects, Hubble must be extremely steady and accurate. The telescope is able to lock onto a target without deviating more than 7/1000th of an arcsecond, or about the width of a human hair seen at a distance of 1 mile.

THE CRAB NEBULA IS A SUPERNOVA REMNANT,
ALL THAT REMAINS OF A TREMENDOUS
STELLAR EXPLOSION. OBSERVERS IN CHINA
AND JAPAN RECORDED THE SUPERNOVA
NEARLY 1,000 YEARS AGO, IN 1054.

THE HEAVENS ARE GOD'S GIANT CANVAS of self-revelation that speaks continuously. There's not a split second of time when there's not a revelation of God in the skies. Every single day. Every single night. Every week. Every year. Ever since they were created. It's 24/7. The heavens are known and seen everywhere. *"The skies proclaim the work of his hands. Day after day they pour forth speech; night after night they display knowledge"* (PSALM 19:1–2 NIV). The skies preach a thousand sermons a day to the human heart. God's revelation in the heavens is also universal. Anyone can see it, and anyone can see it anytime, anywhere. It's inaudible, so anyone can understand it. The heavens don't speak Russian, Chinese, or English. The heavens speak a language everyone can understand. *"There is no speech or language where their voice is not heard. Their voice goes out into all the earth, their words to the ends of the world"* (PSALM 19:3–4).

Today, with our stunning technology, we can read the fine print of God's revelation in the skies and see distant worlds that defy comprehension. God's voice is clearer than ever before. Are we listening? And worshiping? | MARK HITCHCOCK

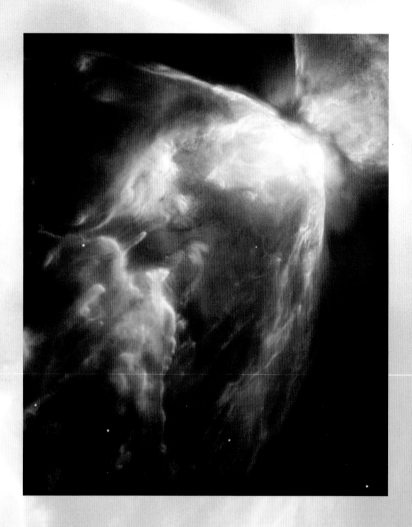

A Dying Star Shrouded by a Blanket of Icy Hailstones Forms the Bug Nebula

(NGC 6302)

He is the living God,

And steadfast forever;

His kingdom is the one which shall not be destroyed,

And His dominion shall endure to the end.

He delivers and rescues,

And He works signs and wonders

In heaven and on earth.

DANIEL 6:26–27

Dying Star Creates Fantasy-like
Sculpture of Gas and Dust

THE CAT'S EYE NEBULA, ONE OF THE FIRST
PLANETARY NEBULAE DISCOVERED, ALSO HAS ONE
OF THE MOST COMPLEX FORMS KNOWN TO THIS
KIND OF NEBULA. ELEVEN RINGS, OR SHELLS, OF
GAS MAKE UP THE CAT'S EYE.

THE CURIOUS WORKMANSHIP OF HEAVEN
SETS FORTH THE GLORY OF ITS MAKER;
THE FIRMAMENT IS BEAUTIFIED
AND PENCILED OUT
IN BLUE AND AZURE COLORS,
WHERE THE POWER AND WISDOM OF GOD
MAY BE CLEARLY SEEN.

THOMAS WATSON

A Body of Divinity

NASA, ESA, HEIC, and The Hubble Heritage Team (STScI/AURA). | Acknowledgment: R. Corradi (Isaac Newton Group of Telescopes, Spain) and Z. Tsvetanov (NASA)

NGC 3603 IS A PROMINENT STAR-FORMING REGION IN THE CARINA SPIRAL ARM OF THE MILKY WAY, ABOUT 20,000 LIGHT-YEARS AWAY. THOUSANDS OF SPARKLING YOUNG STARS ARE NESTLED WITHIN THE GIANT NEBULA. THIS STELLAR "JEWEL BOX" IS ONE OF THE MOST MASSIVE YOUNG STAR CLUS-TERS IN THE MILKY WAY GALAXY.

He counts the number of the stars;
He gives names to all of them.
Great is our Lord and abundant in strength;
His understanding is infinite.

PSALM 147:4–5

GOD IS FRIGHTFULLY POWERFUL, and this is indeed a powerful under-statement. Psalm 33:6 tells us that "By the word of the LORD the heavens were made, and all their host of them by the breath of His mouth." Each of the heavenly host—each twinkling star—is really an unimaginably colossal cauldron of churning and flaming plasma. Our small sun alone could hold over a million earths inside. That there could exist a Being who simply speaks such items into existence is truly a cause for wonder, fear, and humility.

KEVIN HARTNETT

IT TAKES A LOT OF FAITH TO BE AN ATHEIST

because when you look at the complexity of creation,

you certainly see Intelligent design.

The God of the universe is all-powerful and all-knowing.

HE'S EVERYWHERE AT THE SAME TIME.

We bow our heads to pray and He hears

every one of us at the same time.

He made Canis Majoris, He made the earth,

He made the sun, and He made you.

HE LOVES YOU,

AND HE HAS A PLAN AND A PURPOSE FOR YOUR LIFE.

DAVID LANDRITH

Massive Star VY Canis Majoris—
Polarized Light

VY CANIS MAJORIS IS A RED SUPERGIANT STAR THAT

IS ALSO CLASSIFIED AS A HYPERGIANT BECAUSE

OF ITS VERY HIGH LUMINOSITY. IT IS LOCATED 5,000

LIGHT-YEARS AWAY. IT IS 500,000 TIMES BRIGHTER

AND ABOUT 30 TO 40 TIMES MORE MASSIVE THAN

THE SUN. IF THE SUN WERE REPLACED WITH THE

BLOATED VY CANIS MAJORIS, ITS SURFACE COULD

EXTEND TO THE ORBIT OF SATURN.

Hoag's Object Galaxy

A NEARLY PERFECT RING OF HOT, BLUE STARS PINWHEELS ABOUT THE YELLOW NUCLEUS OF AN UNUSUAL GALAXY KNOWN AS HOAG'S OBJECT. THIS IMAGE CAPTURES A FACE-ON VIEW OF THE GALAXY'S RING OF STARS, REVEALING MORE DETAIL THAN ANY EXISTING PHOTO OF THIS OBJECT. THE IMAGE MAY HELP ASTRONOMERS UNRAVEL CLUES ON HOW SUCH STRANGE OBJECTS FORM.

THE ENTIRE GALAXY IS ABOUT 120,000 LIGHT-YEARS WIDE, WHICH IS SLIGHTLY LARGER THAN OUR MILKY WAY GALAXY.

In the words of the apostle Paul,

"God's invisible qualities—his eternal power and divine nature—
have been clearly seen, being understood from what has been made,
so that men are without excuse" (ROMANS 1:20 NIV).

Put another way,

THE ORDER AND COMPLEXITY OF THE UNIVERSE

ELOQUENTLY TESTIFIES TO THE EXISTENCE

OF AN UNCAUSED FIRST CAUSE.

HANK HANEGRAAFF

The Complete Bible Answer Book

Spiral Galaxy NGC 3370

INTRICATE SPIRAL ARMS CONTAIN AREAS OF NEW STAR

FORMATION IN THIS DUSTY GALAXY. THIS GALAXY, WHICH

LIES ABOUT 100 MILLION LIGHT-YEARS AWAY TOWARD THE

DIRECTION OF THE CONSTELLATION LEO, WAS HOME TO A

SUPERNOVA THAT APPEARED IN 1994.

How vital that we pray armed *with the knowledge that God is in heaven.* Pray with any lesser conviction and your prayers are timid, shallow, and hollow. *But spend time walking in the workshop of the heavens, seeing what God has done,* and watch how your prayers are energized.

Max Lucado, *Safe in the Shepherd's Arms*

Twinkle, twinkle, little star,

How I wonder what you are!

Up above the world so high,

Like a diamond in the sky.

When the blazing sun is gone,

When he nothing shines upon,

Then you show your little light,

Twinkle, twinkle, all the night.

Pluto

TWINKLE, TWINKLE, LITTLE STAR,

Then the traveler in the dark,
Thanks you for your tiny spark.
He could not see which way to go,
If you did not twinkle so.

In the dark blue sky you keep,
And often through my curtains peep,
For you never shut your eye,
Till the sun is in the sky.

As your bright and tiny spark,
Lights the traveler in the dark:
Though I know not what you are,
Twinkle, twinkle, little star.

ANN & JUNE TAYLOR

SN 1006 Supernova Remnant

A RIBBON OF GAS, A VERY THIN SECTION OF A SUPERNOVA
REMNANT CAUSED BY A STELLAR EXPLOSION THAT
OCCURRED MORE THAN 1,000 YEARS AGO, FLOATS IN OUR
GALAXY. THE SUPERNOVA THAT CREATED IT WAS PROBABLY
THE BRIGHTEST STAR EVER SEEN BY HUMANS.

GOD HAS MADE EVERYTHING
BEAUTIFUL FOR ITS OWN TIME.
HE HAS PLANTED ETERNITY IN THE
HUMAN HEART, BUT EVEN SO,
PEOPLE CANNOT SEE THE WHOLE
SCOPE OF GOD'S WORK FROM
BEGINNING TO END.

ECCLESIASTES 3:11 NLT

THIS IS AN EXPANDING SHELL OF GLOWING GAS

SURROUNDING A HOT, MASSIVE STAR IN OUR

MILKY WAY GALAXY. ASTRONOMERS HAVE DUBBED

IT THE BUBBLE NEBULA (NGC 7635). THE NEBULA

IS 10 LIGHT-YEARS ACROSS, MORE THAN TWICE

THE DISTANCE FROM EARTH TO THE NEAREST

STAR. ONLY PART OF THE BUBBLE IS VISIBLE IN THIS

IMAGE. THE GLOWING GAS IN THE LOWER RIGHT-

HAND CORNER IS A DENSE REGION OF MATERIAL

THAT IS GETTING BLASTED BY RADIATION FROM

THE BUBBLE NEBULA'S MASSIVE STAR. THE

RADIATION IS EATING INTO THE GAS, CREATING

FINGER-LIKE FEATURES. THIS INTERACTION ALSO

HEATS UP THE GAS, CAUSING IT TO GLOW.

THE GREATNESS OF GOD'S POWER
TO CREATE AND DESIGN AND FORM AND MOLD
AND MAKE AND BUILD AND ARRANGE
DEFIES THE LIMITS OF OUR IMAGINATION.
AND SINCE HE CREATED EVERYTHING,
THERE IS NOTHING BEYOND HIS POWER
TO FIX OR MEND
OR HEAL OR RESTORE.

ANNE GRAHAM LOTZ

My Jesus Is Everything

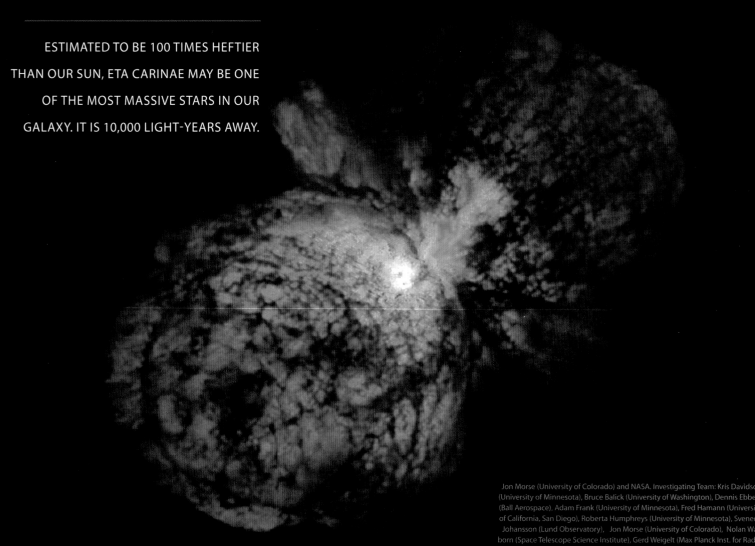

The Doomed Star Eta Carinae

ESTIMATED TO BE 100 TIMES HEFTIER
THAN OUR SUN, ETA CARINAE MAY BE ONE
OF THE MOST MASSIVE STARS IN OUR
GALAXY. IT IS 10,000 LIGHT-YEARS AWAY.

Jon Morse (University of Colorado) and NASA. Investigating Team: Kris Davidso
(University of Minnesota), Bruce Balick (University of Washington), Dennis Ebbe
(Ball Aerospace), Adam Frank (University of Minnesota), Fred Hamann (Universi
of California, San Diego), Roberta Humphreys (University of Minnesota), Svener
Johansson (Lund Observatory), Jon Morse (University of Colorado), Nolan Wa
born (Space Telescope Science Institute), Gerd Weigelt (Max Planck Inst. for Rad
Astronomy, Bonn), and Richard White (Space Telescope Science Institut

GOD'S VOICE IS GLORIOUS

IN THE THUNDER.

WE CAN'T EVEN IMAGINE

THE GREATNESS OF HIS POWER.

JOB 37:5 NLT

Galactic Center Region

THIS IMAGE SHOWS THE CENTER
OF THE MILKY WAY GALAXY.
THE COMPOSITE IMAGE OF
THE GALACTIC CENTER IS
246 LIGHT-YEARS WIDE AND
26,000 LIGHT-YEARS AWAY.

THE BEST REMEDY FOR THOSE WHO ARE AFRAID,

LONELY OR UNHAPPY IS TO GO OUTSIDE,

SOMEWHERE WHERE THEY CAN BE QUIET,

ALONE WITH THE HEAVENS, NATURE AND GOD.

BECAUSE ONLY THEN DOES ONE FEEL THAT

ALL IS AS IT SHOULD BE.

ANNE FRANK

Mars Near Opposition

1995–2005: 2001

AT THE 2005 CLOSEST APPROACH,

MARS WAS 43 MILLION MILES

(69 MILLION KM) FROM EARTH.

WHO IS AS MIGHTY AS GOD? THERE IS NO ONE.

ALL OF THE OCEANS, WORLDS, AND GALAXIES

IN THE INFINITY OF SPACE—

ALL OF THAT RESTS IN THE HAND OF OUR MIGHTY,

OMNISCIENT FATHER WHO HOLDS US, LOVES US,

AND ALWAYS REMINDS US THAT WE ARE HIS.

DR. CHARLES STANLEY

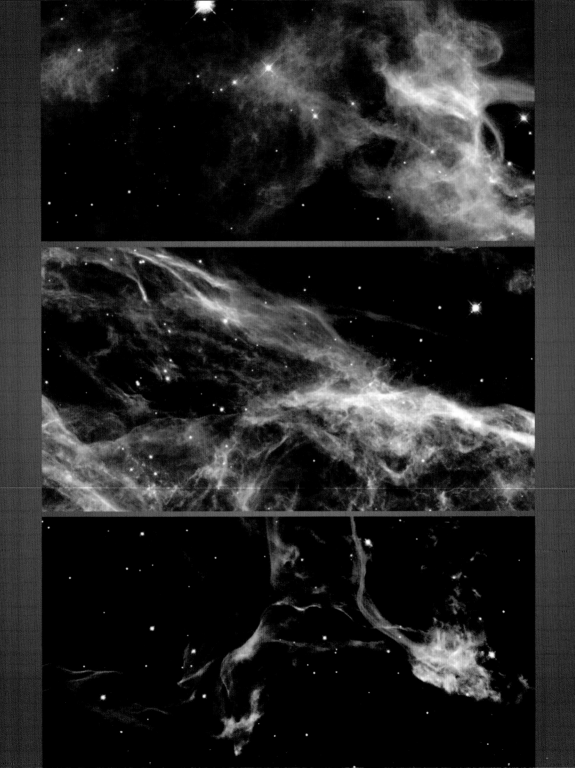

Veil Nebula

NASA'S HUBBLE SPACE TELESCOPE PHOTOGRAPHED THREE MAGNIFICENT SECTIONS OF THE VEIL NEBULA—THE SHATTERED REMAINS OF A SUPER-NOVA THAT HAS EXPLODED. THIS SERIES OF IMAGES PROVIDES BEAUTIFULLY DETAILED VIEWS OF THE DELICATE, WISPY STRUCTURE RESULTING FROM THIS COSMIC EXPLOSION. THE VEIL NEBULA IS ONE OF THE MOST SPECTACULAR SUPERNOVA REMNANTS IN THE SKY. THE ENTIRE SHELL SPANS ABOUT 3 DEGREES ON THE SKY, CORRESPONDING TO ABOUT 6 FULL MOONS.

For by Him all things were created that are in heaven
and that are on earth, visible and invisible,
whether thrones or dominions or principalities or powers.
All things were created through Him and for Him.

COLOSSIANS 1:16

NASA, ESA, and the Hubble Heritage (STScI/AURA)-ESA/Hubble Collaboration; Acknowledgment: J. Hester (Arizona State University)

The Earth has a very special place in the universe. When reading the Book of Genesis, you discover that the Earth takes center stage during the six days of the creation of the universe and all life. In fact, all the heavenly bodies—like the Sun, moon, and stars—were made for signs and seasons for the Earth. Indeed, the Earth is the center of God's attention, and it is where He sent His Son to die on a Cross and then be gloriously resurrected to save us from our sins. Earth is not just an ordinary hunk of rock hanging in space.

However, one of the most influential evolutionists, the late Carl Sagan, said the following just before he died: "We live on a hunk of rock and metal that circles a humdrum star that is one of 400 billion other stars that make up the Milky Way Galaxy, which is one of billions of other galaxies which make up a universe, which may be one of a very large number, perhaps infinite number, of other universes. That is a perspective on human life and culture that is well worth pondering."

What hopelessness—and meaninglessness—in that declaration! Yet what purpose and meaning we find in the declaration from Genesis: "In the Beginning, God created the heavens and the Earth," and then on Day 6, He created man in His image. | KEN HAM

He has made the earth BY HIS POWER,

He has established the WORLD BY HIS WISDOM,

And has stretched out the heavens AT HIS DISCRETION.

JEREMIAH 10:12

ARP 148

ARP 148 IS THE STAGGERING AFTERMATH OF AN
ENCOUNTER BETWEEN TWO GALAXIES, RESULTING
IN A RING-SHAPED GALAXY AND A LONG-TAILED
COMPANION. THE COLLISION BETWEEN THE TWO
PARENT GALAXIES PRODUCED A SHOCKWAVE EFFECT
THAT FIRST DREW MATTER INTO THE CENTER AND
THEN CAUSED IT TO PROPAGATE OUTWARDS IN A
RING. ARP 148 IS NICKNAMED MAYALLS OBJECT AND
IS LOCATED IN THE CONSTELLATION OF URSA MAJOR,
THE GREAT BEAR, APPROXIMATELY 500 MILLION
LIGHT-YEARS AWAY.

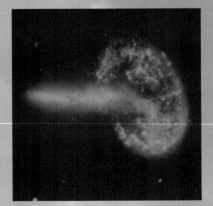

I imagine God looking through the artistry

of His heavens to this little ball called Earth,

zooming in through the chaos and noise and turmoil

and activity, and focusing in on my heart.

As the universe rages and rotates around Him,

He has the grace and love to care what happens to me.

How can that be?

TERRI BLACKSTOCK

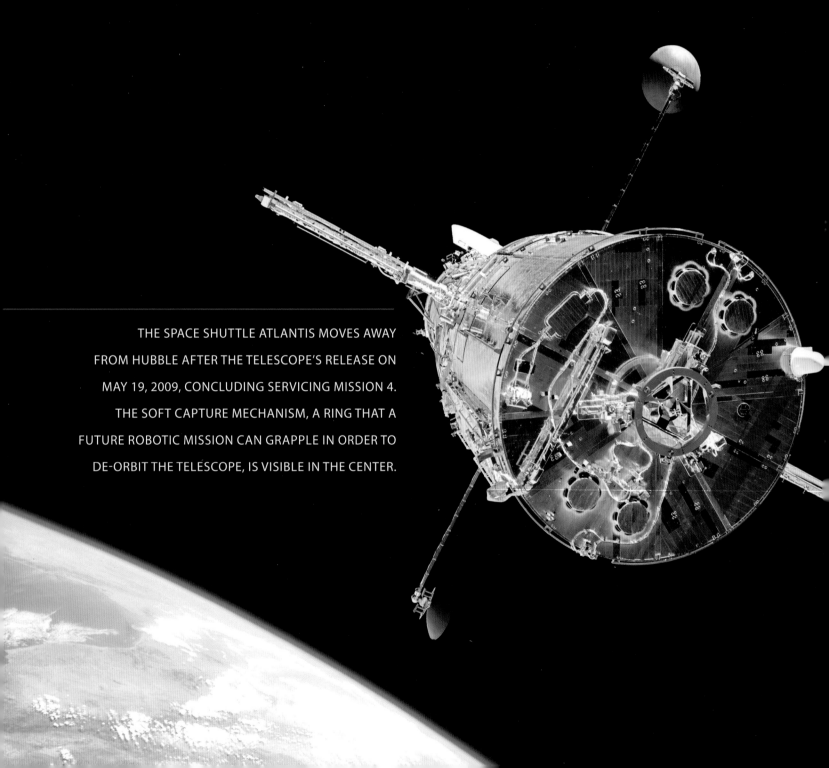

THE SPACE SHUTTLE ATLANTIS MOVES AWAY FROM HUBBLE AFTER THE TELESCOPE'S RELEASE ON MAY 19, 2009, CONCLUDING SERVICING MISSION 4. THE SOFT CAPTURE MECHANISM, A RING THAT A FUTURE ROBOTIC MISSION CAN GRAPPLE IN ORDER TO DE-ORBIT THE TELESCOPE, IS VISIBLE IN THE CENTER.

In order to create a Hubble image, technicians must schedule each observation down to a fraction of a second. Observation information—such as which instrument to use, what filter to use, and how long the exposure should be—must be converted into a detailed technical list of second-by-second instructions. These instructions are loaded onto the telescope's computers a few days before the scheduled observation.

The raw data collected by the telescope have a long way to go before they become actual Hubble images. As Hubble completes a particular observation, it converts the starlight into digital signals. The digital signals are then relayed down to a ground station at White Sands, New Mexico through two orbiting Tracking and Data Relay Satellites (TDRS). The ground station then relays the data to Goddard Space Flight Center's ground control system, where staff ensure its completeness and accuracy.

Goddard then sends the data via data lines to the Space Telescope Science Institute for processing and calibration. Institute personnel translate the data into scientifically meaningful units—such as wavelength or brightness—and archive the information on 5.25-inch (13.3-cm) magneto-optical disks. Hubble sends the archive enough information to fill about 18 DVDs every week. Astronomers can download archived data via the Internet and analyze it from anywhere in the world.

The Glowing Eye of Planetary Nebula NGC 6751

GLOWING IN THE CONSTELLATION AQUILA
LIKE A GIANT EYE, THE NEBULA IS A CLOUD OF
GAS EJECTED FROM THE HOT STAR VISIBLE IN
ITS CENTER. PLANETARY NEBULA ARE SHELLS
OF GAS THROWN OFF BY STARS OF MASSES
SIMILAR TO THAT OF OUR OWN SUN, WHEN

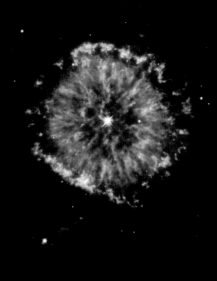

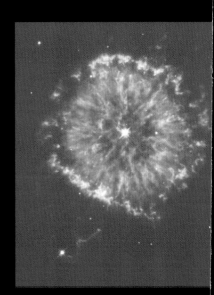

THE NIGHT SKY IN SOUTHERN CALIFORNIA IS ESPECIALLY BEAUTIFUL.

God's handprint in His creation is on grand display even to the unaided eye.

While some scientists view the universe through a fractured worldview lens,

claiming to see it as the result of a celestial accident, other esteemed scientists recognize

that God alone created and continues to rule the universe. God's Word bears the original

witness to that truth in both the Old and New Testaments where we read:

"In the beginning God created the heavens and the earth. . . .

In the beginning was the Word, and the Word was with God, and the Word was God.

He was in the beginning with God. All things were made through Him,

and without Him nothing was made that was made" (GENESIS 1:1; JOHN 1:1–3).

That same amazing God of creation is the God of our salvation

and is our eternal hope in this chaotic world.

DAVID JEREMIAH

beta pictoris

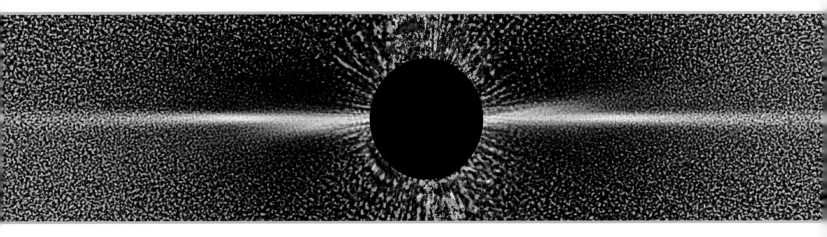

BETA PICTORIS IS LOCATED 63 LIGHT-YEARS AWAY

IN THE SOUTHERN CONSTELLATION PICTOR.

ALTHOUGH THE STAR IS MUCH YOUNGER THAN THE SUN,

IT IS TWICE AS MASSIVE AND NINE TIMES MORE LUMINOUS.

Believing in a supernatural, creative God who

made everything is the only possible rational explanation

for the universe and for life itself.

It is also the only basis for believing we have any purpose or destiny.

By faith we understand that the worlds were framed

by the word of God, so that the things which are seen

were not made of things which are visible (HEBREWS 11:3).

JOHN MACARTHUR, *Battle for the Beginning*

The Dusty Galaxy NGC 1316

LIKE DUST BUNNIES THAT LURK IN CORNERS AND UNDER BEDS, SURPRISINGLY

COMPLEX LOOPS AND BLOBS OF COSMIC DUST LIE HIDDEN IN THE GIANT

ELLIPTICAL GALAXY NGC 1316. THIS IMAGE MADE FROM DATA OBTAINED WITH

THE NASA HUBBLE SPACE TELESCOPE REVEALS THE DUST LANES AND STAR

CLUSTERS OF THIS GIANT GALAXY THAT GIVE EVIDENCE THAT IT WAS FORMED

FROM A PAST MERGER OF TWO GAS-RICH GALAXIES.

"THIS IS WHAT THE LORD SAYS—

your Redeemer, who formed you in the womb:

I am the LORD,

who has made all things,

who alone stretched out the heavens,

who spread out the earth by myself."

ISAIAH 44:24 NIV

NASA, ESA, and the Hubble Heritage Team (STScI/AURA). | Acknowledgment: P. Goudfrooij (STScI)

When have you observed the blazing glory

of a tropical sunset or the soft, silvery shimmer of moonlight on the ocean waves, or a baby's birth and first lusty cry, or a bird weaving her nest, hatching and feeding her young . . . and wondered, *who made it?*

When we thoughtfully consider the world around us, we instinctively know our environment is not some haphazard cosmic accident but the handiwork of a Master Designer. The earth did not come about by the snap of some giant fingers but was deliberately planned and prepared in an orderly progression of events. Like planet Earth around us, our lives are not a haphazard cosmos, either. They were deliberately planned to be filled with the beauty of love and joy and peace and purpose-filled— with God Himself. | ANNE GRAHAM LOTZ, *God's Story*

Combined X-Ray and Optical Images of the Crab Nebula

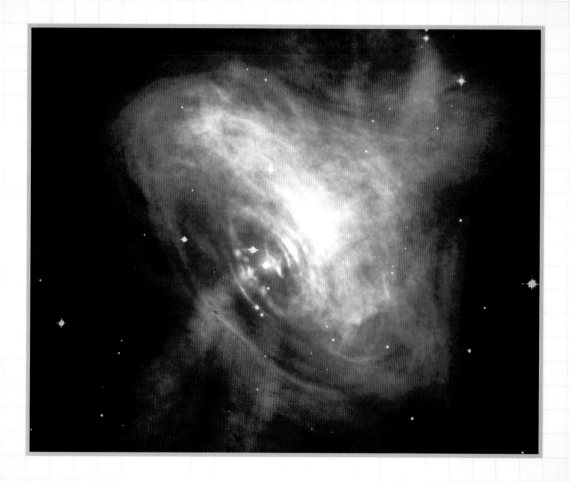

Your mercy is great above the heavens,
And Your truth reaches to the clouds.

PSALM 108:4

Star Clusters Born Among the Interacting Galaxies of Stephan's Quintet

THIS CLOSE-UP VIEW OF STEPHAN'S QUINTET, A GROUP OF FIVE GALAXIES, REVEALS A STRING OF BRIGHT STAR CLUSTERS THAT SPARKLES LIKE A DIAMOND NECKLACE. THE CLUSTERS, EACH HARBORING UP TO MILLIONS OF STARS, WERE BORN FROM THE VIOLENT INTERACTIONS BETWEEN SOME MEMBERS OF THE GROUP. THE RUDE ENCOUNTERS ALSO HAVE DISTORTED THE GALAXIES' SHAPES, CREATING ELONGATED SPIRAL ARMS AND LONG, GASEOUS STREAMERS. IT IS APPROXIMATELY 280,000 LIGHT-YEARS IN VERTICAL DIRECTION.

Physics professors say it's true: a butterfly can flap its wings, setting in motion molecules of air that move other molecules of air, that in turn move additional molecules—eventually influencing weather patterns on the other side of the planet. Likewise, a single individual—even in the vastness of space that the Hubble shows us—can have this kind of butterfly effect and impact people on the other side of a century marker, across cultures, and around the globe. Yes, you matter. You who are made of dust and are a speck too tiny to be located on a Hubble photo, nevertheless matter to the Creator of these galaxies!

ANDY ANDREWS

He alone is your God, the only one
who is worthy of your praise,
the one who has done these mighty miracles
that you have seen with your own eyes.

DEUTERONOMY 10:21 NLT

NASA, Jayanne English (University of Manitoba), Sally Hunsberger (Pennsylvania State University), Zolt Levay (Space Telescope Science Institute), Sarah Gallagher (Pennsylvania State University), and Jane Charlton (Pennsylvania State University) | Science Cre dits: Sarah Gallagher (Pennsylvania State University), Jane Charlton (Pennsylvania State University), Sally Hunsberger (Pennsylvania State University), Dennis Zaritsky (University of Arizona), and Bradley Whitmore (Space Telescope Science Institute)

The Changing Faces of Pluto

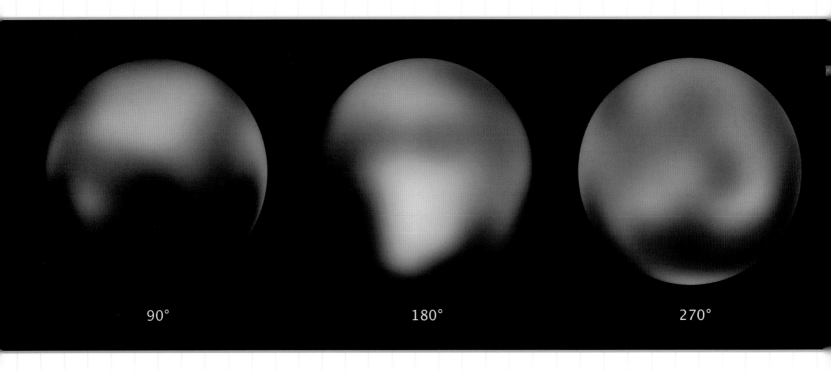

90°   180°   270°

THIS IS THE MOST DETAILED VIEW TO DATE OF THE ENTIRE SURFACE OF THE DWARF PLANET PLUTO,
AS CONSTRUCTED FROM MULTIPLE NASA HUBBLE SPACE TELESCOPE PHOTOGRAPHS TAKEN
FROM 2002 TO 2003. THIS SERIES OF PICTURES TOOK FOUR YEARS AND 20 COMPUTERS OPERATING
CONTINUOUSLY AND SIMULTANEOUSLY TO ACCOMPLISH.

THERE IS IN GOD *all that may draw*

forth both wonder and delight;

there is a constellation of all beauties;

HE IS . . . THE ORIGINAL AND SPRINGHEAD OF BEING,

who sheds a glory upon His children.

THOMAS WATSON

A Body of Divinity

Polar Ring Galaxy NGC 4650A

THE EXTRAORDINARY "POLAR-RING" GALAXY NGC 4650A IS LOCATED ABOUT 130 MILLION LIGHT-YEARS AWAY, AND IT IS ONE OF ONLY 100 KNOWN POLAR-RING GALAXIES. THEIR UNUSUAL DISK-RING STRUCTURE IS NOT YET UNDERSTOOD FULLY. ONE POSSIBILITY IS THAT POLAR RINGS ARE THE REMNANTS OF COLOSSAL COLLISIONS BETWEEN TWO GALAXIES SOMETIME IN THE DISTANT PAST.

Who has gone up to heaven and come down?
Who has gathered up the wind in the hollow of his hands?
Who has wrapped up the waters in his cloak?
Who has established all the ends of the earth?
What is his name, and the name of his son?
Tell me if you know!

PROVERBS 30:4 NIV

THIS IS A THRILLING PASSAGE OF SCRIPTURE. As an evangelist, my heart races

to answer the question from the pages of the Bible: . . .

"The Lord Almighty

is His name . . .

the Redeemer . . .

the God of all the earth."

ISAIAH 54:5 NIV

As I look at this astounding photograph taken by the Hubble telescope,
a cross-like image comes into view. God proclaimed and promised:
"I will show wonders in the heaven above and signs on the earth below . . .
Everyone who calls on the name of the Lord will be saved" (ACTS 2:19, 21 NIV).
"I, when I am lifted up from the earth, will draw all men to myself" (JOHN 12:32 NIV).
"I will . . . bring my salvation to the ends of the earth" (ISAIAH 49:6 NIV).
This is exactly what the God of heaven and earth did—
He orchestrated the most excruciating rescue mission of all time by sending
salvation down from heaven in the form of His only beloved Son, the Lord Jesus.
God said, *"It is I who made the earth and created mankind upon it. My own hands*
stretched out the heavens; I marshaled their starry hosts" (ISAIAH 45:12 NIV).
The Son of God stretched His arms out for all people to demonstrate
His mercy and love for the whole world.
He took our sins and covered them with His crimson blood in death.
But He rose from the grave, conquered death
and lives victorious in the realm of Glory.
"Let them praise the name of the LORD, for his name alone is exalted;
his splendor is above the earth and the heavens" (PSALM 148:13 NIV).

FRANKLIN GRAHAM

3C 321: Galaxy Fires at Neighboring Galaxy

THIS COMPOSITE IMAGE SHOWS THE JET FROM A BLACK HOLE AT
THE CENTER OF A GALAXY STRIKING THE EDGE OF ANOTHER GALAXY.
THE JET IMPACTS THE COMPANION GALAXY AT ITS EDGE AND IS THEN
DISRUPTED AND DEFLECTED.

WE KNOW THAT GOD IS EVERYWHERE;
but certainly we feel His presence most when His works
are on the grandest scale spread before us:
and it is in the unclouded night-sky,
where His worlds wheel their silent course,
that we read clearest
HIS INFINITUDE, HIS OMNIPOTENCE, HIS OMNIPRESENCE.

CHARLOTTE BRONTË, *Jane Eyre*

black hole

Planetary Nebula NGC 2818

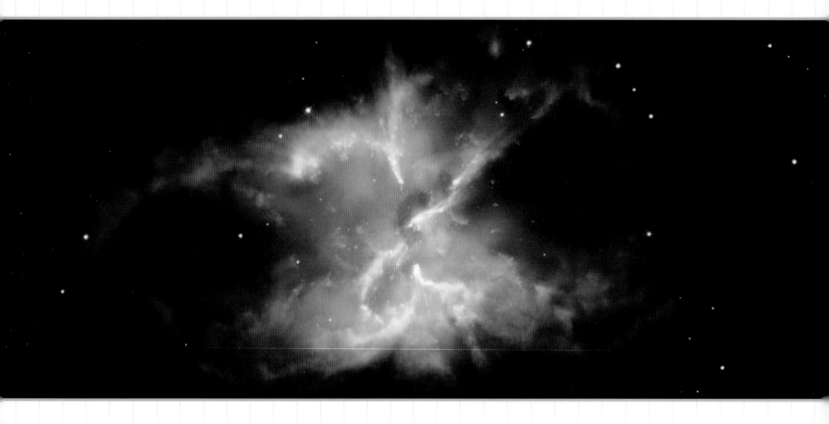

THIS IS THE FAMED PLANETARY NEBULA DESIGNATED NGC 2818, WHICH LIES IN THE SOUTHERN CON-STELLATION OF PYXIS (THE COMPASS). THE SPECTACULAR STRUCTURE OF THE PLANETARY NEBULA CONTAINS THE OUTER LAYERS OF A STAR THAT WERE EXPELLED INTO INTERSTELLAR SPACE. PLANETARY NEBULAE HAVE BEEN DETECTED IN SEVERAL GLOBULAR STAR CLUSTERS IN OUR GALAXY. THESE ARE DENSELY PACKED, GRAVITATIONALLY BOUND GROUPS OF 100,000s TO MILLIONS OF STARS.

When I come to die, I want someone there

with me who is stronger than death.

I want to walk through the door of eternity

with the Creator of the Universe,

Life Incarnate,

God who became man,

died for me,

defeated the grave,

and calls me His friend.

You can have all this world, just give me Jesus.

KIRK CAMERON

Hubble/IRTF Composite Image
of Jupiter Storms

THE TENDENCY IN SO MANY *of us is to reduce God to a personally useful deity.* The vision of God's great glory so powerfully on display in this unique book drew me to "look up" and *worship such a magnificent God* rather than "look in" and expect Him to do my bidding. *It's a wonderful reminder for people of all ages.*

DR. LARRY CRABB

Interacting Galaxy Pair Arp 87

TWO GALAXIES SWING PAST EACH OTHER IN A GRACEFUL PERFORMANCE CHOREOGRAPHED BY GRAVITY. THIS IS ONE OF HUNDREDS OF INTERACTING AND MERGING GALAXIES KNOWN IN OUR NEARBY UNIVERSE.

How vast is Your creation?

What great power in the Word You spoke

that brought the universe into being?

When I see Your works, Lord,

I cannot help but bow

with all of nature to worship You.

STORMIE OMARTIAN

Hubble-Spitzer Color Mosaic of the Galactic Center

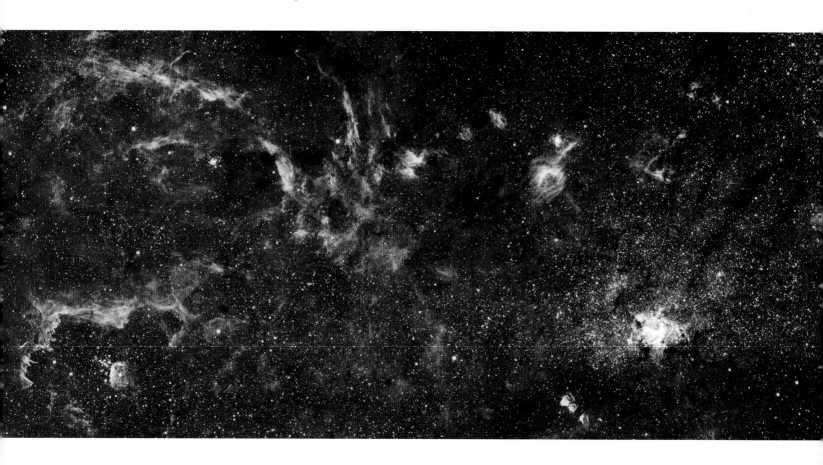

THIS SWEEPING PANORAMA IS THE SHARPEST INFRARED PICTURE EVER MADE

OF THE MILKY WAY'S GALACTIC CORE, WHERE MASSIVE STARS ARE FORMING.

You need a Yahweh.

You need a God who can place 100 billion stars
in our galaxy and 100 billion galaxies in the universe.
You need a God who can shape two fists of flesh into 75 to 100
billion nerve cells, each with as many as 10,000 connections
to other nerve cells, place it in a skull, and call it a brain.
You need a God who can come in the soft of night and
touch you with the tenderness of April snow.

You need a Yahweh.

MAX LUCADO, *Safe in the Shepherd's Arms*

Hubble Observes Infant Stars
in Nearby Galaxy

THIS CLUSTER IS WITHIN A STAR-FORMING
REGION IN THE SMALL MAGELLANIC CLOUD.
IT IS APPROXIMATELY 196,000
LIGHT-YEARS AWAY.

IN A FRESH, ASTOUNDING WAY, THIS BOOK

has caused my head to bow,

my knees to bend,

my will to yield,

my hands to serve,

my mind to worship,

and my heart to fall in love all over again

with the One whose glory

is revealed in the heavens!

ANNE GRAHAM LOTZ

Hubble's Festive View of a Grand Star-Forming Region

A HUBBLE PICTURE POSTCARD, TAKEN OCTOBER 20–27, 2009, SHOWS HUNDREDS OF BRILLIANT BLUE STARS WREATHED BY WARM, GLOWING CLOUDS. THE FESTIVE PORTRAIT IS THE MOST DETAILED VIEW OF THE LARGEST STELLAR NURSERY IN OUR LOCAL GALACTIC NEIGHBORHOOD. MANY OF THE DIAMOND-LIKE ICY BLUE STARS ARE AMONG THE MOST MASSIVE STARS KNOWN. SEVERAL OF THEM ARE OVER 100 TIMES MORE MASSIVE THAN OUR SUN. IT IS LOCATED 170,000 LIGHT-YEARS AWAY AND IS A MEMBER OF THE LOCAL GROUP OF GALAXIES, WHICH ALSO INCLUDES THE MILKY WAY.

He is the Creator of the universe and the Designer

of the human body. He is the Author of salvation history and the Sovereign over world history. He sits enthroned as the ultimate Victor over sin, death, and pain. He keeps planets in their orbits . . . . and your heart beating.

Yet this Almighty God, enthroned in the heavens, bends down to listen to the entreaty of one of His children. It's amazing that our Almighty God has any thoughts at all toward His creatures. But consider what the psalmist said: "Your thoughts which are toward us cannot be recounted to You in order; if I would declare and speak of them, they are more than can be numbered" (PSALM 40:5). The fact that God's thoughts toward us are innumerable is more than we can fathom.

God sits exalted above the universe. We are weak and needy creatures. Yet the Lord thinks of us, hears our cries, brings us up out of horrible places, sets our feet on rock, and puts a song of praise in our mouths (vv. 1–3). He is our Help and our Deliverer. Go to Him now with praise!

HENRY AND RICHARD BLACKABY, *Discovering God's Daily Agenda*

Light Echo from Star V838 Monocerotis

Now to Him who is able to keep you from stumbling,

And to present you faultless

Before the presence of His glory with exceeding joy,

To God our Savior,

Who alone is wise,

Be glory and majesty,

Dominion and power,

Both now and forever.

Amen.

JUDE 1:24–25

As Your children gather in peace

All the angels sing in Heaven

In Your temple all that I seek

Is to glimpse Your holy presence

All the heavens cannot hold You, Lord

How much less to dwell in me?

I can only make my one desire

Holding on to Thee

ALL THE ANGELS EXALT YOU ON HIGH

What a kingdom to depart!

But You left Your throne in the sky

JUST TO LIVE INSIDE MY HEART

All the heavens cannot hold You, Lord

How much less to dwell in me?

I will always make my one desire

Holding on to Thee

THIRD DAY, "ALL THE HEAVENS"

The Colorful Demise of a Sun-like Star

NASA, ESA, and K. Noll (STScI) | Acknowledgment: The Hubble Heritage Team (STScI/AURA)

"We give You thanks,

O Lord God Almighty,

The One who is and who was

and who is to come,

Because You have taken

Your great power and reigned."

REVELATION 11:17

ASTRONAUT JOHN GRUNSFELD PERFORMS WORK
ON THE HUBBLE SPACE TELESCOPE AS THE FIRST OF
FIVE SPACEWALKS ON MAY 14, 2009, KICKED OFF A
WEEK OF WORK ON THE ORBITING OBSERVATORY.
GRUNSFELD, A SPACEWALK VETERAN WITH A LONG
RELATIONSHIP WITH THE TELESCOPE, PARTICIPATED
IN THREE SPACEWALKS DURING SERVICING
MISSION 4.

Hubble Servicing Mission 4 took place in May 2009. It is expected to extend Hubble's life into at least 2013. A rejuvenated telescope will continue to beam images of the heavens back to Earth, transferring about 120 gigabytes of data every week.

Hubble's successor, the James Webb Space Telescope (JWST), is currently in the works. JWST will study objects from the earliest universe, objects whose light has "redshifted," or stretched into infrared light.

From its orbit 940,000 miles (1.5 million km) away from Earth, JWST will unveil secrets about the birth of stars, solar systems, and galaxies by peering through the dust that blocks visible light. The telescope is scheduled to launch in 2014.

Eventually, Hubble's time will end. As the years progress, Hubble's components will slowly degrade to the point at which the telescope stops working.

When that happens, Hubble will continue to orbit Earth until its orbit decays, allowing it to spiral toward Earth. Though NASA originally hoped to bring Hubble back to Earth for museum display, the telescope's prolonged lifespan has placed it beyond the date for the retirement of the space shuttle program. Hubble was designed specifically to function with the space shuttle, so the replacement vehicle will likely not be able to return it to the ground. A robotic mission is expected to help de-orbit Hubble, guiding its remains through a plunge through the atmosphere and into the ocean.

But Hubble's legacy—its discoveries, its trailblazing design, its success in showing us the universe in unparalleled detail—will live on. Scientists will rely on Hubble's revelations for years as they continue in their quest to understand the cosmos—a quest that has attained clarity, focus, and triumph through Hubble's rich existence.

Grateful acknowledgment
is given to all who participated in making this book possible.

NAMES ARE LISTED IN THE ORDER OF APPEARANCE IN THIS BOOK.

ANNE GRAHAM LOTZ. Anne Graham Lotz is founder of AnGeL Ministries and is an award-winning and bestselling author. Excerpts in this book were taken from: *God's Story* © 2009 by Anne Graham Lotz (Nashville, TN: Thomas Nelson, Inc.), pages 1–2 and Prologue. Used with permission. *Just Give Me Jesus* © 2009 by Anne Graham Lotz (Nashville, TN: Thomas Nelson, Inc.), Pages 8 and 10. Used with permission. Quotes without reference were written for this book and were used with permission. Visit her Web site at www.annegrahamlotz.com. *Thank you to all at AnGeL Ministries who prayed over this project.*

KEVIN HARTNETT. Kevin Hartnett is NASA's Deputy Science Operations Manager for the Hubble Space Telescope and works at the Goddard Space Flight Center in Greenbelt, MD. You can read more of his beautiful poetry and devotions at khartnettpoetry.typepad.com. Page 7, © May 1997, page 25, © January 2000, page 49, © July 2002, page 62, © December 2001, page 105, © July 2002. Used with permission.

JOHN MACARTHUR. John MacArthur is a bestselling author, pastor-teacher of Grace Community Church, president of Master's College and Seminary, and president of Grace to You. His excerpts were taken from *Battle for the Beginning* (Nashville, TN: Thomas Nelson, Inc., © 2005 by John MacArthur), pp 37, 45, 105, 117. Used with permission.

MAX LUCADO. Max Lucado is Minister of Preaching for the Oak Hills Church in San Antonio, Texas. He is the husband of Denalyn and father of Jenna, Andrea, and Sara. In a good week he reads a good book, has a few dinners with his wife, and breaks 90 on the golf course. He usually settles for the first two. Excerpts by Max were taken from *Hope Pure & Simple*, *The Great House of God*, and *Safe in the Shepherd's Arms*. Used with permission.

MAX LUCADO. Max Lucado is Minister of Preaching for the Oak Hills Church in San Antonio, Texas. He is the husband of Denalyn and father of Jenna, Andrea, and Sara. In a good week he reads a good book, has a few dinners with his wife, and breaks 90 on the golf course. He usually settles for the first two. Excerpts by Max were taken from *Hope Pure & Simple*, *The Great House of God*, and *Safe in the Shepherd's Arms*. Used with permission.

FRANCIS CHAN. Francis Chan, *Crazy Love* © 2008 Cook Communications Ministries/David C. Cook. Crazy Love by Francis Chan. Used with permission. Permission required to reproduce. All rights reserved. Pp 26 and 28.

SARAH YOUNG. Sarah Young is the bestselling author of *Jesus Calling*, *Jesus Lives*, *Dear Jesus*, and *Jesus Calling: 365 Devotions for Kids*. Sarah and her husband have traveled the world planting churches and counseling. They currently are ministering to a Japanese-speaking community in Australia.

THOMAS WATSON. All quotes by Thomas Watson are from *A Body of Divinity Hardcover Edition* (Jay P. Green, Sr., 2002) pp 5, 7, and 16.

DR. RICHARD LEE. Dr. Richard Lee is the founding pastor of First Redeemer Church in Atlanta. *There's Hope, America*, his radio/television ministry is broadcast nationwide in 42 million homes across the U.S. and in 17 countries. He is also the author of the bestselling *American Patriots Bible*.

HANK HANEGRAAFF. Hank Hanegraaff is president and chairman of the board for Christian Research Institute. He is also host of *Bible Answer Man* radio program and is the author of several award-winning, bestselling books. Excerpts are from *The Complete Bible Answer Book, Collector's Edition* (Nashville, TN: Thomas Nelson, Inc. © 2009). Used with permission.

R. C. SPROUL. R. C. Sproul is an American Calvinist theologian and pastor. He is the founder and chairman of Ligonier Ministries and can be heard daily on the *Renewing Your Mind* radio. He is the author of more than sixty books and has served as general editor of *The Reformation Study Bible*. Visit his Web site at www.oneplace.com.

STEPHEN MANSFIELD. Stephen Mansfield is the *New York Times* bestselling author of *The Faith of Barack Obama*, and *Never Give In*. For more information about Stephen, log onto www.mansfieldgroup.com.

NETA JACKSON. Neta Jackson is author of *The Yada Yada Prayer Group* and *The Yada Yada House of Hope* novels. To find out more about Neta and her books, go to www.daveneta.com.

ROBERT MORGAN. Robert Morgan is the pastor of The Donelson Fellowship in Nashville, Tennessee, and a bestselling Gold-Medallion winning writer with over 20 books in print. Visit his Web site at www.robertjmorgan.com.

AUSTIN GUTWEIN. At the age of nine, Austin Gutwein organized a free-throw marathon to raise funds for children orphaned by HIV/AIDS. Since then his organization, Hoops of Hope, has raised over a million dollars to build a high school and medical clinic in Zambia. Read more about his amazing story in *Take Your Best Shot* and visit his Web site at www.hoopsofhope.org.

FRANK PERETTI. Frank Peretti's first novel, *This Present Darkness*, spent over 150 consecutive weeks on the CBA Bestseller List. Following novels like *The Oath*, *The Visitation*, *Monster*, and *House* have opened the public's eye to the supernatural thriller. Learn more by visiting his Web site at www.frankperetti.com.

Homer Hickam. Homer Hickam is author of bestselling *Rocket Boys*, the book from which Universal Studios produced the film *October Sky*. During his NASA career, Mr. Hickam trained astronaut crews for many Spacelab and Space Shuttle missions, including the Hubble Space Telescope deployment mission, and the first two Hubble repair missions. Visit his Web site at www.homerhickam.com.

Joni Eareckson Tada. Joni Eareckson Tada is founder of "Joni and Friends," a ministry that reaches out to people who are disabled and suffering and to those who care for them. She can be heard daily on the Christian Radio across the country. Visit her Web site at www.joniandfriends.org.

Mike Huckabee. Mike Huckabee served as the 44th Governor of Arkansas from 1996–2007. He is the host of "Huckabee" on the Fox News Channel, and the "Huckabee Report" on the Citadel Media Network. He is also author of 6 books. Visit his Web site at www.mikehuckabee.com.

Patsy Clairmont. Patsy Clairmont is an original Women of Faith speaker, with a quick wit and depth of biblical knowledge making a powerful pint-size package. She is also the author of the bestselling books *God Uses Cracked Pots*, *Normal is Just a Setting on Your Dryer*, *Sportin' a 'Tude*, and many more. Check out her latest book *Kaleidoscope: Seeing God's Wit and Wisdom in a Whole New Light* and her Web site at www.patsyclairmont.com.

Sheila Walsh. Sheila Walsh is author of the award-winning *Gigi, God's Little Princess* series for girls, as well as multiple books for women, including *The Heartache No One Sees* and *Good Morning, Lord* devotional. She is also a regular speaker for Women of Faith. Visit her Web site at www.sheilawalsh.com.

Fernando Ortega. "Jesus, King of Angels" by Fernando Ortega © 1998 Margeedays Music (Admin. by Dayspring Music, LLC), Dayspring Music, LLC. All rights reserved. Used by permission.

Ken Ham. Ken Ham is president and founder of Answers in Genesis U.S. and the new highly acclaimed Creation Museum in Petersburg, Kentucky. Ken is heard daily on the radio feature *Answers . . . with Ken Ham* and is a frequent guest on national TV talk-show programs. Visit his Web site at www.answersingenesis.org.

Jack & Marsha Countryman. Jack Countryman is founder of JCountryman, the original name for the Gift Division of Thomas Nelson. He is the creator and bestselling author of the God's Promises® line, with over 9 million books in print. Marsha is Jack's "Rock of Gibraltar" and loving wife of 45 years.

Mark Hitchcock. Mark Hitchcock is a leading Bible prophecy expert, prolific author (with over 20 books) on the end times, senior pastor of Faith Bible Church in Edmond, Oklahoma, and adjunct faculty member of the Dallas Theological Seminary. Visit his Web site at www.marklhitchcock.com.

David Landrith. David Landrith has been senior pastor of Long Hollow Baptist Church, in Hendersonville, Tennessee since 1997. His quote was taken from his sermon titled "Authentic Worship" from the All In series. You can listen to or watch the sermon at www.longhollow.com. Used with permission.

Dr. Charles Stanley. Dr. Charles Stanley is senior pastor of First Baptist Church in Atlanta, GA. He is also the founder and president of In Touch® Ministries and a *New York Times* bestselling author. His radio and television broadcast, "In Touch with Dr. Charles Stanley," can be heard around the globe, in every nation and in more than 50 languages. Visit his Web site at www.intouch.org.

Terri Blackstock. Terri Blackstock has over thirty Christian titles in print, many of which have been #1 bestsellers. Learn more about Terri by visiting www.terriblackstock.com.

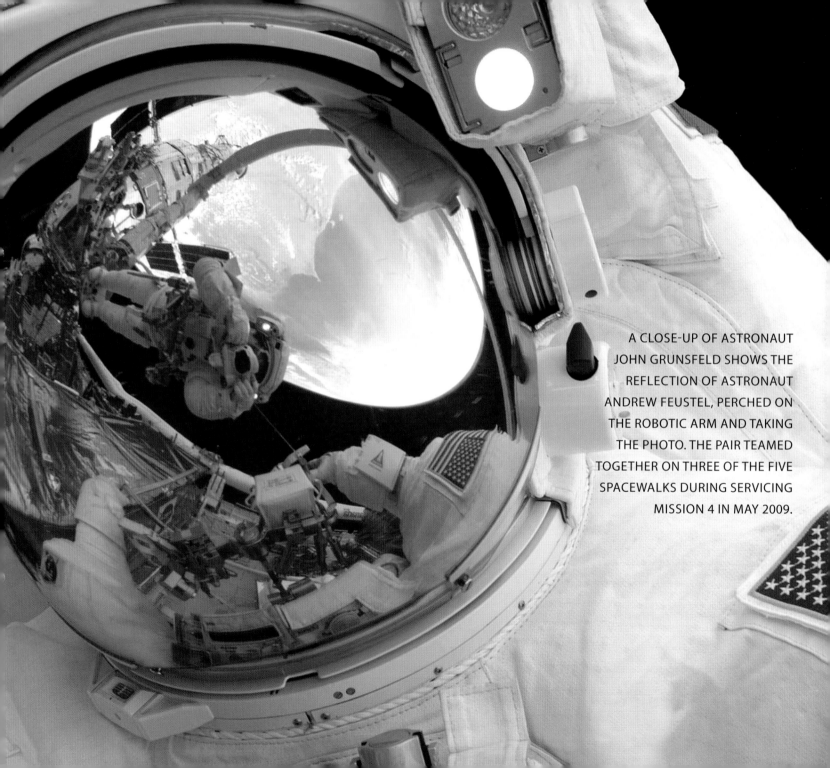

A CLOSE-UP OF ASTRONAUT JOHN GRUNSFELD SHOWS THE REFLECTION OF ASTRONAUT ANDREW FEUSTEL, PERCHED ON THE ROBOTIC ARM AND TAKING THE PHOTO. THE PAIR TEAMED TOGETHER ON THREE OF THE FIVE SPACEWALKS DURING SERVICING MISSION 4 IN MAY 2009.

ANDY ANDREWS. Andy Andrews is *New York Times* best-selling author of *The Noticer* and *The Traveler's Gift*, inspirational speaker, and passionate fisherman. Find out more about Andy at www.andyandrews.com.

FRANKLIN GRAHAM. Franklin Graham is president and CEO of the Billy Graham Evangelistic Association and president and CEO of Samaritan's Purse. Visit his Web site at www.samaritanspurse.org.

KIRK CAMERON. Kirk Cameron is best known for his role in *Growing Pains* (1985–1992). He's also starred in *Fireproof* and the *Left Behind* films. He co-hosts the spiritually based reality show *The Way of the Master* and is founder of Camp Firefly, a camp for seriously ill children and their families. Visit his Web site at www.kirkcameron.com.

DR. LARRY CRABB. Dr. Larry Crabb is a well-known psychologist, conference and seminar speaker, Bible teacher, popular author, and founder/director of NewWay Ministries. Visit his Web site at www.newwayministries.org.

STORMIE OMARTIAN. Stormie Omartian is the bestselling author of *The Power of Praying* series and is in high demand as an international speaker. Learn more about Stormie at www.stormieomartian.com.

DR.'s HENRY AND RICHARD BLACKABY. Dr. Henry Blackaby is the founder and president emeritus of Blackaby Ministries International and is author of the bestselling book *Experiencing God*. Dr. Richard Blackaby has served as the president of Blackaby Ministries International since July 2006. He has also co-authored numerous books with his father Henry. Excerpts were taken from *Discovering God's Daily Agenda* (Nashville, TN: Thomas Nelson, Inc. © 2007 by Dr's Richard and Henry Blackaby), page 319. Used with permission.

THIRD DAY. "All the Heavens" by Tai Anderson / Brad Avery / David Carr / Mark Lee / Mac Powell. Copyright © 2000 Vandura 2500 Songs (ASCAP) (adm. by EMI CMG Publishing) / New Spring Publishing (ASCAP). All rights reserved. Used by permission. © 2000 NEW SPRING PUBLISHING/VANDURA 2500 SONGS. All Rights Reserved.

> IN ADDITION TO THE HUBBLE IMAGES, "ALL THE HEAVENS" INSPIRED THE CONCEPT OF THIS BOOK. THANK YOU, THIRD DAY, FOR WRITING AND SINGING THIS SONG!

NASA. *Thank you* to the hundreds of scientists, engineers, and technicians at the Goddard Space Flight Center, the Space Telescope Science Institute (STScI), AURA, NICMOS Science Team, ESA, SSC, CXC, ST-ECF, and the numerous individuals who bear the collective responsibility for operating the Hubble Space Telescope, for monitoring its health, safety, and performance, and for creating the spectacular images we are now able to enjoy.